CHILDREN'S ISSUES, LAWS AND PROGRAMS

STATE CHILDREN'S HEALTH INSURANCE PROGRAM

ELEMENTS AND CONSIDERATIONS

CHILDREN'S ISSUES, LAWS AND PROGRAMS

Additional books in this series can be found on Nova's website under the Series tab.

Additional e-books in this series can be found on Nova's website under the e-book tab.

CHILDREN'S ISSUES, LAWS AND PROGRAMS

STATE CHILDREN'S HEALTH INSURANCE PROGRAM

ELEMENTS AND CONSIDERATIONS

MARTY SPARKS
EDITOR

nova publishers
New York

Library of Congress Cataloging-in-Publication Data

ISBN: 978-1-63483-675-3

Published by Nova Science Publishers, Inc. † New York

CONTENTS

PREFACE

The State Children's Health Insurance Program (CHIP) is a means-tested program that provides health coverage to targeted low-income children and pregnant women in families that have annual income above Medicaid eligibility levels but have no health insurance. CHIP is jointly financed by the federal government and states, and the states are responsible for administering CHIP. Under the CHIP program, the federal government sets basic requirements for CHIP, but states have the flexibility to design their own version of CHIP within the federal government's basic framework. As a result, there is significant variation across CHIP programs. This book describes the basic elements of CHIP, focusing on how the program is designed, who is eligible, what services are covered, how enrollees share in the cost of care, and how the program is financed. The book also includes a brief discussion of the future of CHIP. Furthermore, this book examines provisions of H.R. 2, which is the Medicare Access and CHIP Reauthorization Act (MACRA) of 2015; CHIP financing, beginning with an explanation of the federal matching rate; and the ACA MOE requirement for children if federal CHIP funding expires.

In: State Children's Health Insurance Program ISBN: 978-1-63483-675-3
Editor: Marty Sparks

Chapter 1

STATE CHILDREN'S HEALTH INSURANCE PROGRAM: AN OVERVIEW*

Evelyne P. Baumrucker and Alison Mitchell

SUMMARY

The State Children's Health Insurance Program (CHIP) is a means-tested program that provides health coverage to targeted low-income children and pregnant women in families that have annual income above Medicaid eligibility levels but have no health insurance. CHIP is jointly financed by the federal government and states, and the states are responsible for administering CHIP. In FY2013, CHIP enrollment totaled 8.4 million individuals and CHIP expenditures totaled $13.2 billion.

Under the CHIP program, the federal government sets basic requirements for CHIP, but states have the flexibility to design their own version of CHIP within the federal government's basic framework. As a result, there is significant variation across CHIP programs. Currently, state upper-income eligibility limits for children range from a low of 175% of the federal poverty level (FPL) to a high of 405% of FPL. States may also extend CHIP coverage to pregnant women when certain conditions are met.

States may design their CHIP programs in three ways: a CHIP Medicaid expansion, a separate CHIP program, or a combination

---

* This is an edited, reformatted and augmented version of a Congressional Research Service publication R43627, prepared for Members and Committees of Congress, dated April 23, 2015.

approach where the state operates a CHIP Medicaid expansion and one or more separate CHIP programs concurrently. CHIP benefit coverage and cost-sharing rules depend on program design. CHIP Medicaid expansions must follow the federal Medicaid rules for benefits and cost sharing, which entitles CHIP enrollees to Early and Periodic Screening, Diagnostic, and Treatment (EPSDT) coverage (effectively eliminating any state-defined limits on the amount, duration, and scope of any benefit listed in Medicaid statute) and exempts the majority of children from any cost sharing. For separate CHIP programs, the benefits are permitted to look more like private health insurance, and states may impose cost sharing, such as premiums or enrollment fees, with a maximum allowable amount that is tied to annual family income.

The federal government reimburses states for a portion of every dollar they spend on CHIP (including both CHIP Medicaid expansions and separate CHIP programs) up to state-specific annual limits called allotments. The federal share of FY2013 total expenditures was $9.2 billion and the state share was $4.0 billion.

CHIP was enacted in 1997. Since that time, Congress has extended federal CHIP funding. The Patient Protection and Affordable Care Act (ACA; P.L. 111-148, as amended) extended CHIP funding through FY2015. On April 16, 2015, President Obama signed into law the Medicare Access and CHIP Reauthorization Act of 2015 (MACRA; P.L. 114-10). MACRA repeals the sustainable growth rate (SGR) mechanism (which overrides the reduction in the Medicare physician fee schedule that was set to begin in April 2015) and extends funding for CHIP, among other provisions. Specifically, MACRA extends CHIP funding for two additional years (i.e., through FY2017) and maintains the current allotment formula, including a 23 percentage point increase to the enhanced federal medical assistance percentage (E-FMAP). MACRA also extends the "qualifying state" option, the Child Enrollment Contingency Fund, "Express Lane" eligibility, Outreach and Enrollment Grants, the Pediatric Quality Measures Program, and the Childhood Obesity Demonstration Project.

Although MACRA adds two additional years to federal funding for CHIP (through FY2017), states still need to adhere to the ACA's maintenance of effort (MOE) requirements that are in effect through FY2019. The MOE requires states to maintain income eligibility levels for CHIP children through September 30, 2019, as a condition for receiving federal Medicaid payments (notwithstanding the lack of corresponding federal CHIP appropriations for FY2018 and FY2019). The MOE requirements impact CHIP Medicaid expansion programs and separate CHIP programs differently.

- *For CHIP Medicaid expansion programs*, when federal CHIP funding is exhausted, the CHIP-eligible children in these programs continue to be enrolled in Medicaid but financing switches from CHIP to Medicaid.

- *For separate CHIP programs*, states are provided a couple of exceptions to the MOE: (1) after September 1, 2015, states may enroll CHIP-eligible children into qualified health plans in the health insurance exchanges or (2) states may impose waiting lists or enrollment caps in order to limit CHIP expenditures. In addition, in the event that a state's CHIP allotment is insufficient to fund CHIP coverage for all eligible children, a state must establish procedures to screen children for Medicaid eligibility, and enroll those who are Medicaid-eligible. For children not eligible for Medicaid, the state must establish procedures to enroll CHIP children in qualified health plans in the health insurance exchanges that have been certified by the Secretary of Health and Human Services (HHS) to be "at least comparable" to CHIP in terms of benefits and cost sharing.

Congress will face a decision with regard to the future of CHIP when federal CHIP funding expires after FY2017. If Congress does not act and federal CHIP funding ends, some CHIP enrollees likely would continue to have coverage through Medicaid as a result of the MOE requirements, but others would need to find another source of health insurance coverage (e.g., employer-sponsored health insurance or through the health insurance exchanges), and some likely would be uninsured. Congress's action or inaction on the CHIP program may affect health insurance options and resulting coverage for targeted low-income children that are eligible for the current CHIP program.

This report describes the basic elements of CHIP, focusing on how the program is designed, who is eligible, what services are covered, how enrollees share in the cost of care, and how the program is financed. The report ends with a brief discussion of the future of CHIP.

INTRODUCTION

The State Children's Health Insurance Program (CHIP) is a federal-state program that provides health coverage to certain uninsured low-income children and pregnant women in families that have annual income above Medicaid eligibility levels, but have no health insurance. CHIP is jointly financed by the federal government and states, and the states are responsible for administering CHIP. Participation in CHIP is voluntary and all states, the District of Columbia, and the territories[1] participate. The federal government sets basic requirements for CHIP, but states have the flexibility to design their own version of CHIP within the federal government's basic framework. As a result, there is significant variation across CHIP programs.

CHIP was established as part of the Balanced Budget Act of 1997 (BBA 97; P.L. 105-33) under a new Title XXI of the Social Security Act (SSA). Since that time, other federal laws have provided additional funding, and made significant changes to CHIP. Most notably, the Children's Health Insurance Program Reauthorization Act of 2009 (CHIPRA; P.L. 111-3) increased appropriation levels for CHIP, and changed the formula for allotments (i.e., federal funds allocated to each state for the federal share of their CHIP expenditures), eligibility, and benefit requirements.[2] The Patient Protection and Affordable Care Act (ACA; P.L. 111-148, as amended) largely maintains the current CHIP structure through FY2019. The law also extends federal appropriations through FY2015 and requires states to maintain their Medicaid and CHIP child eligibility levels through FY2019 as a condition for receiving Medicaid federal matching funds.[3]

On April 16, 2015, President Obama signed into law the Medicare Access and CHIP Reauthorization Act of 2015 (MACRA; P.L. 114-10). MACRA repeals the sustainable growth rate (SGR) mechanism (which overrides the reduction in the Medicare physician fee schedule that was set to begin in April 2015) and extends funding for CHIP, among other provisions. Specifically, MACRA extends CHIP funding for two additional years (i.e., through FY2017) and maintains the current allotment formula with the 23 percentage point increase to the enhanced federal medical assistance percentage (E-FMAP). MACRA also extends the "qualifying state" option, the Child Enrollment Contingency Fund, "Express Lane" eligibility, Outreach and Enrollment Grants, the Pediatric Quality Measures Program, and the Childhood Obesity Demonstration Project.[4]

Congress will face a decision with regard to the future of CHIP when federal CHIP funding expires after FY2017. The health insurance market is far different today than when CHIP was established. CHIP was designed to work in coordination with Medicaid to provide health coverage to low-income children.[5] In general, CHIP allows states to cover CHIP children with no health insurance in families with annual income above state Medicaid eligibility levels. Before CHIP was established, no federal program provided health coverage to children with family with annual incomes above Medicaid eligibility levels. The ACA further expanded the options for children in certain low-income families with incomes above CHIP eligibility levels by offering subsidized coverage for insurance purchased through health insurance exchanges. Congress's action or inaction on the CHIP program will affect the health insurance options available to targeted low-income children and their resulting health coverage.

This report describes the basic elements of CHIP, focusing on how the program is designed, who is eligible, what services are covered, how enrollees share in the cost of care, and how the program is financed. The report ends with a brief discussion of the future of CHIP.

PROGRAM DESIGN

States may design their CHIP programs in three ways. They may cover eligible children under their Medicaid programs (i.e., CHIP Medicaid expansion),[6] create a separate CHIP program, or adopt a combination approach where the state operates a CHIP Medicaid expansion and one or more[7] separate CHIP programs concurrently.[8] In all cases, federal CHIP funding is available to pay for the costs for services provided to CHIP children.[9]

State choices for program design impact the coverage that enrollees receive. When states provide Medicaid coverage to CHIP children (i.e., CHIP Medicaid expansion), Medicaid rules (Title XIX of SSA) typically apply. When states provide coverage to CHIP children through separate CHIP programs, Title XXI of SSA rules typically apply. States that want to make changes to their programs beyond what both laws allow may seek approval from the Centers for Medicare and Medicaid Services (CMS) through the use of the Section 1115 waiver authority.[10]

Where relevant, differences between Title XIX and Title XXI of the SSA program rules regarding eligibility, benefit coverage, cost sharing and financing are summarized in Table 1, and highlighted throughout the report.

Table 1. Key Differences in Federal Rules Regarding Selected Program Features Between CHIP Medicaid Expansion Programs and Separate CHIP Programs

Program Feature Eligibility	CHIP Medicaid Expansion	Separate CHIP Program
Who is eligible?	CHIP children are an optional eligibility group in Medicaida and enrollees must be covered statewide.	Eligibility may vary based on geography, age, annual family income, residency, disability status, access to other health insurance, and duration of CHIP eligibility.

Table 1. (Continued)

Program Feature Eligibility	CHIP Medicaid Expansion	Separate CHIP Program
Entitlement Nature Implications of the ACA maintenance of effort (MOE)[c]	Individual Entitlement[b] When federal CHIP funding is exhausted, CHIP Medicaid expansion children must continue to be enrolled in Medicaid through September 30, 2019, but the financing switches from CHIP to Medicaid.	Not an individual entitlement. States with separate CHIP programs are provided with exceptions to the MOE. When federal CHIP funding is exhausted, states must establish procedures to screen and enroll eligible children in Medicaid. For children not eligible for Medicaid, the state must establish procedures to enroll CHIP children in qualified health plans in the health insurance exchanges that have been certified by the Secretary of Health and Human Services (HHS) to be "at least comparable" to CHIP in terms of benefits and cost sharing. If there are no certified plans, the MOE does not obligate states to provide coverage to these children.
Benefits	CHIP children are entitled to Early and Periodic Screening, Diagnostic, and Treatment (EPSDT) coverage, which effectively eliminates any state-defined limits on the amount, duration, and scope of any benefit listed in Medicaid statute.	States have more latitude in designing their benefit coverage.
Cost Sharing	Premiums and cost sharing are generally prohibited for CHIP children under age 18.	In general, premiums and cost- sharing may be imposed. Allowable amounts are dependent on annual family income and are subject to an out-of-pocket

Program Feature Eligibility	CHIP Medicaid Expansion	Separate CHIP Program
		aggregate limit of 5% of annual family income.
Financing Entitlement Nature	Capped entitlement to states appropriated through FY2017.	Capped entitlement to states appropriated through FY2017.
Federal matching rate	Based on Enhanced-Federal Medical Assistance Percentage (E-FMAP) Rate.d	Based on Enhanced-Federal Medical Assistance Percentage (E-FMAP) Rate.[d]

Source: CRS analysis of Titles XIX and XXI of the Social Security Act.

Notes: CHIP gives states the flexibility to design their programs as an expansion of Medicaid or as a separate CHIP program, or to adopt a combination approach where the state operates a CHIP Medicaid expansion and one or more separate CHIP programs concurrently. State choices for program design have implications for the federal government, states and beneficiaries. Key differences across various program features are summarized in this table.

[a] §1902(gg)(2) includes a Medicaid maintenance of effort (MOE) that requires continuous eligibility standards for Medicaid eligible children (including CHIP Medicaid expansion children) through September 30, 2019, as a condition of receiving federal Medicaid funding.

[b] Under Medicaid, individuals who meet the program eligibility requirements and enroll in the program are guaranteed Medicaid coverage.

[c] The ACA CHIP MOE (§2105(d)(3)) requires states to maintain income eligibility levels for CHIP through September 30, 2019, as a condition for receiving payments under Medicaid (notwithstanding the lack of corresponding federal appropriations for FY2018 and FY2019).

[d] The federal government funds a larger share of CHIP expenditures than Medicaid. From FY2016 through FY2019, the E-FMAP is set to increase by 23 percentage points (not to exceed 100%) for most CHIP expenditures.

As of July 1, 2014, 8 states, the District of Columbia, and the territories had CHIP Medicaid expansions, 13 states had separate CHIP programs,[11] and 29 states used a combination approach.[12] (See Appendix A, Table A-1 for 50-state information on CHIP program design.) FY2013 state-reported CHIP enrollment data (the most recent data available) show that the bulk of CHIP enrollees received coverage through separate CHIP programs (approximately 70%). The remainder received coverage through a CHIP Medicaid expansion.[13] This enrollment distribution has largely held true over the course of the program's history (see Figure 1 below). However, this landscape likely will change due to modifications to CHIP eligibility rules enacted under the

ACA. (For more information on these and other eligibility related requirements, see the "Eligibility" subsection.) Preliminary FY2014 CHIP enrollment data show about half of CHIP enrollees are in CHIP Medicaid expansion programs and about half are in separate CHIP programs.[14]

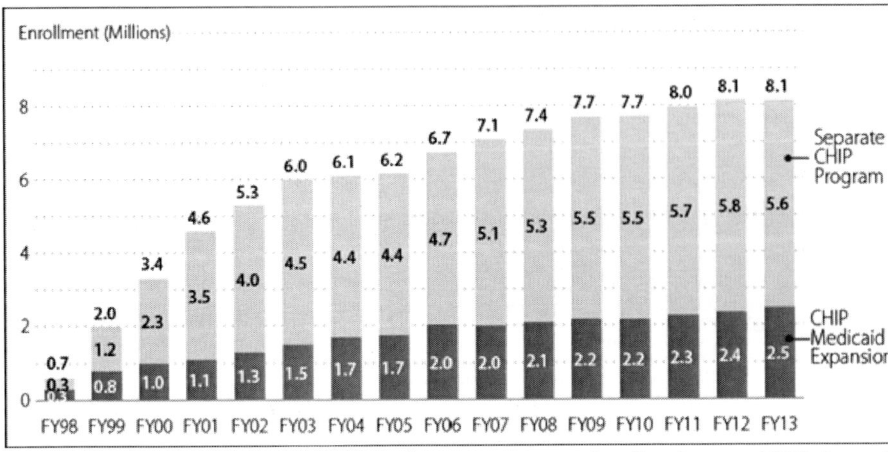

Source: CHIP child enrollment counts by program type for fiscal years 1998 through 2011 are from MACPAC, Overview of Medicaid and CHIP, January 2013. FY2012 CHIP child enrollment counts by program type are from MACPAC, Report to the Congress on Medicaid and CHIP, March 2013, and FY2013 enrollment counts are from MACPAC, Report to the Congress on Medicaid and CHIP, March 2014.

Notes: Data are reported by individual states and are representative of children ever enrolled in Medicaid and CHIP as of a specified date. States may subsequently revise their current and/or historical data.

Figure 1. Number of Children Ever Enrolled in CHIP by Program Type, FY1998-FY2013.

ELIGIBILITY

This section describes CHIP eligibility rules. In general, CHIP extends coverage to certain low-income children and pregnant women without health insurance in families with annual family income too high to qualify them for Medicaid. Specifically, Title XXI of the SSA defines a targeted low-income child as one who is under age 19 with no health insurance,[15] and who would not have been eligible for Medicaid under the federal and state rules in effect when CHIP was first initiated in 1997.[16] (Hereinafter, targeted low-income children are referred to as CHIP children, CHIP-eligible or CHIP-enrolled, as applicable.) States have broad discretion in setting their income eligibility standards, and eligibility varies across states. Children under age 19 represent the vast majority of CHIP program enrollment.[17]

Children

CHIP Medicaid Expansions

States with a CHIP Medicaid expansion program must follow the eligibility rules of the Medicaid program (See Table 1). Because CHIP eligibility builds on top of Medicaid eligibility, the Medicaid child eligibility rules that were in effect when CHIP was established in 1997 represent the Medicaid eligibility ceiling for children.[18]

States with CHIP Medicaid expansion programs may cover CHIP children by expanding their Medicaid programs in the following ways: (1) by establishing a new optional eligibility group for such children as authorized in Title XXI of SSA, and/or (2) by liberalizing the financial rules for any of several existing Medicaid eligibility categories. Many states with CHIP Medicaid expansion programs chose the latter, opting to cover CHIP children under existing Medicaid eligibility pathways, especially Medicaid's poverty-related child groups, rather than by establishing the Title XXI of SSA optional coverage group. Such a strategy reduces the administrative burden of creating and implementing a new coverage group.[19] Regardless of the state's approach, CHIP children are an optional eligibility group in Medicaid and enrollees must be covered statewide.

Separate CHIP Programs

States are permitted to determine the eligibility criteria for the group of CHIP children who may enroll in separate CHIP programs (See Table 1).[20] Title XXI of the SSA allows states to use the following factors in determining eligibility: geography (e.g., sub-state areas or statewide), age (e.g., subgroups under 19), income, residency, disability status (so long as any standard relating to disability status does not restrict eligibility),[21] access to or coverage under other health insurance (to establish whether such access/coverage precludes CHIP eligibility),[22] and duration of CHIP eligibility (states must re-determine eligibility at least annually).[23]

States can set the upper income level for CHIP children up to 200% of the federal poverty level (FPL), or 50 percentage points above the applicable pre-

CHIP Medicaid income level. However, prior to January 1, 2014, states were able to use income disregards,[24] which effectively permitted states to expand eligibility to children under age 19 at whatever level they chose. Two states, New Jersey, and New York, plus one California county used this income-counting methodology[25] to expand their CHIP programs to 355% FPL, 405% FPL, and 416% FPL, respectively.[26] The income-disregard option was eliminated under the ACA.

CHIP Eligibility Changes Under the ACA

Beginning January 1, 2014, the ACA required the federal government and states to rely on modified adjusted gross income (MAGI)[27] income counting rules when determining eligibility for CHIP[28] as well as most of Medicaid's nonelderly populations[29] and subsidized exchange coverage. Under the MAGI rules, a state looks at each individual's MAGI, deducts 5% (which the law provides as a standard disregard), and compares that income to the new income standards set by each state. The transition to MAGI effectively limits CHIP upper income eligibility levels for states by eliminating a state's ability to use income disregards to extend coverage to children in families at higher income levels.[30] Also under the ACA, states are permitted to use CHIP federal matching funds to cover children who lose Medicaid eligibility as a result of the elimination of income disregards.[31]

As a part of a separate provision, the ACA required states to transition CHIP "stairstep" children aged 6 through 18 in families with annual income less than 133% FPL (based on MAGI) to Medicaid, beginning January 1, 2014.[32] According to a recent Medicaid budget survey, 21 states transitioned children from CHIP to Medicaid in 2014 as a result of this requirement.[33] Of the states impacted by this policy, another study estimates that on average 28% (or approximately 562,000 stairstep children) made this transition in January 2014.[34] The purpose of this transition was to ensure uniform child coverage under Medicaid up to 133% FPL (effectively 138% after adjustment for the 5% disregard) across all states.

The ACA also required states to maintain income eligibility levels for CHIP through September 30, 2019, as a condition for receiving payments under Medicaid (notwithstanding the lack of corresponding federal appropriations for FY2018 and FY2019).[35] This provision is often referred to as the ACA Maintenance of Effort (MOE) requirement. (Implications of the MOE requirement for the future of CHIP are discussed in more detail in the financing section below.)

Upper Income Eligibility Levels in CHIP

Statewide upper income eligibility thresholds for CHIP-funded child coverage vary substantially across states, ranging from a low of 175% FPL to a high of 405% FPL. Appendix A, Table A-1 shows state-reported child upper income eligibility levels based on MAGI (adjusted for the 5% disregard), as of January 1, 2014.

To summarize, Table A-1 shows:

- 18 states and the District of Columbia provide coverage above 301% FPL; of these, two states extend coverage above 400% FPL, including New York (405% FPL) and California (416% FPL[36] in one county);
- 9 states provide coverage between 251% FPL and 300% FPL;
- 20 states provide coverage between 201% FPL and 250% FPL; and
- 3 states extend coverage at levels less than 200% FPL, including Idaho (190% FPL), North Dakota (175% FPL), and Arizona (100%).[37]

Despite the fact that 27 states extend CHIP coverage to children in families with annual income greater than or equal to 251% FPL, CMS administrative data show that CHIP enrollment is concentrated among families with annual income at lower levels. FY2013 state-reported administrative data show that approximately 89% of CHIP child enrollees were in families with annual income at or below 200% FPL, and approximately 97% of child enrollees were in families with annual income at or below 250% FPL. (See Table 2.) Families with higher income levels are more likely to have access to employer-sponsored insurance coverage.[38] With the enactment of the ACA, families may also have access to subsidized coverage through the exchange. However, such coverage is not always affordable for low-income families. (For more information on the definition of affordability of employer-sponsored insurance coverage as it relates to a family's ability to qualify for subsidized exchange coverage, see the discussion of the "family glitch issue" in the subsection entitled "The Future of CHIP.")

Table 2. Number of Children Ever Enrolled in CHIP by Income Level, FY2013

Income Range (% FPL)	Ever Enrolled	Percentage
0-200	7,243,295	88.5%
201 - 250	724,785	8.9%
251 - 300	165,120	2.0%
301 & Higher	51,791	0.6%
Total	8,184,991	100.0%

Source: Centers for Medicare and Medicaid Services, Child Health Insurance Program Budget Report, based on Form 21E and 64.21E Combined, as of April 2014.
FPL: Federal poverty level.

Figure B-1 through Figure B-4 of Appendix B show the 50-state upper income eligibility levels for children and pregnant women in Medicaid, CHIP, and subsidized exchange coverage, as of January 1, 2014. Variability exists across states in the income eligibility ranges (i.e., income eligibility floors and ceilings) associated with each of the programs. The federal Medicaid statute establishes mandatory coverage floors (defined as a percentage of the federal poverty level) for its poverty-related pregnant women and children eligibility pathways. However, states are permitted to extend Medicaid coverage above these federal minimum levels; this is why there is variability across states in terms of the income eligibility levels at which CHIP begins. For example, the state of Alabama extends Medicaid eligibility to infants in families with annual income less than or equal to 141% FPL, while the state of Iowa extends Medicaid eligibility to infants in families with annual income less than or equal to 240% FPL. In another example, CHIP coverage for children extends to a higher income eligibility threshold than subsidized health insurance exchange coverage in one county in California and in the state of New York (i.e., 416% FPL[39] and 405% FPL, respectively).

It is important to note, however, that not all children with family income at the specified levels are eligible for each of the programs due to program rules that differ for each of these programs. For instance, CHIP is only available to uninsured children, subsidized exchange coverage is not available to individuals with access to minimum essential coverage,[40] and insurance status is not considered when determining Medicaid eligibility.

These figures show both the range of CHIP income eligibility relative to the other programs, and how the programs are envisioned to work together in extending coverage to low-income children and families. CHIP in some states covers a relatively small segment of the income eligibility continuum while CHIP in other states covers a larger segment of the continuum. This is particularly true for infants and pregnant woman. States have used the optional Medicaid eligibility pathways to set higher Medicaid income eligibility levels for infants and pregnant women relative to older children (see Figure B-1 through Figure B-4 of Appendix B). As a result, CHIP has been used to provide health coverage to older uninsured children to a greater extent.

In general, the Medicaid program is a much larger program than CHIP. Child enrollment in Medicaid, for example, was 38.7 million as compared to 8.1 million in CHIP in FY2013.[41] The figures in Appendix B, however, are *not* weighted to reflect program enrollment by state. For example, it is possible that a state with a large uninsured child population but a CHIP program with a relatively narrow income eligibility range may result in a much larger number of CHIP program enrollees than a state with a relatively small uninsured child population and a CHIP program with a much broader income eligibility range.[42]

Pregnant Women and Unborn Children

Nineteen states provide coverage to pregnant women under CHIP. The three main ways that states may extend CHIP coverage to pregnant women (regardless of their age) are through (1) the state plan option for pregnant women; (2) the Section 1115 waiver authority; and/or (3) the unborn child pathway.[43] The latter is the predominant pathway used by states for this purpose.

As of January 2014, four states (Colorado, New Jersey, Oregon, and Rhode Island) extended coverage to pregnant women under Section 1115 waiver authority or the CHIP pregnant women state plan option.[44] Under CHIPRA, states are permitted to cover pregnant women through a state plan amendment[45] when certain conditions are met (e.g., the Medicaid income standard for pregnant women must be at least 185% FPL but in no case lower than the percentage level in effect on July 1, 2008; no preexisting conditions or waiting periods may be imposed; and CHIP cost-sharing protections apply). The period of coverage associated with the state plan option includes pregnancy through the postpartum period (roughly through 60 days postpartum), and benefits include all services available to CHIP children in the state as well as prenatal, delivery, and postpartum care. Infants born to such pregnant women are deemed eligible for Medicaid or CHIP, as appropriate, and are covered up to age one year.

As of January 2014, 15 states provide CHIP coverage to pregnant women ages 19 and older by extending coverage to unborn children as permitted through federal regulation. Coverage available to such women may be limited to prenatal and delivery services, but is still used in 15 states because it permits the extension of CHIP coverage to a pregnant woman regardless of her immigration status.[46] See Figure B-4 for state-specific CHIP eligibility levels for unborn children, pregnant women and deemed newborns, as of January 1, 2014.

BENEFITS

CHIP Medicaid Expansions

As is the case with eligibility, CHIP benefit coverage depends on program design (see Table 1). States that use CHIP Medicaid expansion programs must provide CHIP-eligible children with the full range of mandatory Medicaid benefits, as well as all optional services that the state chooses to cover as specified in their state Medicaid plans.[47] As an alternative to providing all of the mandatory and selected optional benefits under traditional Medicaid, states may enroll state-specified groups, including children in CHIP Medicaid expansions, in Alternative Benefit Plans (ABPs).[48] When certain conditions are met, states may also provide premium assistance for health insurance offered through private insurance arrangements for Medicaid children (including CHIP children) and their parents.

For CHIP children, benefits available through Medicaid's Early and Periodic Screening, Diagnostic, and Treatment (EPSDT) Program *must* be provided, whether through traditional state plan coverage or otherwise. The EPSDT program covers health screenings and services, including assessments of each child's physical and mental health development; laboratory tests (including lead blood level assessment); appropriate immunizations; health education; and vision, dental, and hearing services. States are required to provide all federally allowed treatment to correct problems identified through screenings. EPSDT sets Medicaid benefit coverage for children (including CHIP children) apart from other sources of health insurance in that it permits coverage of all services listed in Medicaid statute (regardless of whether a given benefit is covered in the state plan) and it effectively eliminates any state-defined limits on the amount, duration, and scope of this benefit.

Separate CHIP Programs

States that offer separate CHIP programs have more latitude in designing their programs.[49] Such states are allowed to determine which services to cover, and may place limits on the services that they offer.

Separate CHIP program rules permit states to elect any of three benefit options:[50]

1. Benchmark benefit package: includes one of the following three base benchmark plans:
   - the standard Blue Cross/Blue Shield preferred provider option offered under the Federal Employees Health Benefits Program (FEHBP),
   - the health coverage that is offered and generally available to state employees in the state involved, and/or
   - health coverage that is offered by a health maintenance organization (HMO) with the largest commercial (non-Medicaid) enrollment in the state involved.
2. Benchmark-equivalent coverage: defined as a package of benefits that has the same actuarial value51 as one of the base benchmark benefit packages listed above. A state choosing to provide benchmark-equivalent coverage must cover each of the benefits in the "basic benefits category," including inpatient and outpatient hospital and physicians' surgical and medical services, lab, x-ray, and well-baby and well-child care, including age-appropriate immunizations. Benchmark-equivalent coverage must also include at least 75% of the actuarial value of coverage under the benchmark plan for each of the benefits in the "additional service category." These additional services include prescription drugs, vision services, and hearing services. States are encouraged to cover other categories of service not listed above; and/or
3. Secretary-approved coverage: defined as any other health benefits plan that the Secretary of Health and Human Services (HHS) determines will provide appropriate coverage to the targeted population of uninsured children.[52]

Regardless of the choice of program design, all states must cover emergency services, well baby and well child care including age-appropriate immunizations, and dental services.[53] If offered, mental health services must meet federal mental health parity requirements.[54] As with Medicaid, abortions cannot be covered, except in the case of a pregnancy resulting from rape or incest, or when an abortion is necessary to save the mother's life. Finally, when certain conditions are met (e.g., CHIP minimum benefits and CHIP cost-sharing protections), states can also offer premium assistance to pay a beneficiary's share of costs for group (employer-based) health insurance for CHIP children and their parents.[55] According to a recent study of CHIP benefit coverage, 11 states offered premium assistance programs with CHIP federal matching funds in 2013.[56]

Data from this study that looked at benefit coverage in 42 separate CHIP programs (in 38 states) indicate that in 2013:

- 25 states chose Secretary-approved coverage;
- 9 states offered benchmark-equivalent coverage;
- 3 states offered coverage available in the largest HMO in the state;
- 3 states offered existing state-based coverage;
- 1 state offered FEHBP-equivalent coverage; and
- 1 state offered state employee coverage.

According to this study, benefits offered under separate CHIP programs ranged from benefit coverage modeled after the state's Medicaid plan[57] to more limited benefit coverage available through the commercial market. The study also found that coverage for basic medical services (e.g., physician, hospital, laboratory and radiological services) were largely covered without "significant" limitations. States did impose limitations on other types of services (e.g., physical, occupational and speech therapy; orthodontia; hearing aids; and corrective lenses). Finally, only a few services were not covered at all (e.g., care coordination for children with special needs, non-emergency medical transportation).[58]

In FY2013, managed care was the predominant delivery system under CHIP. Administrative data show that approximately 84% of separate CHIP enrollees received coverage under some form of managed care, while the remaining 16% received coverage under a fee-for-service arrangement.[59]

Cost Sharing

As with eligibility and benefits, cost-sharing rules depend on a state's CHIP program design (See Table 1). Cost sharing refers to the out-of-pocket payments made by beneficiaries of a health insurance plan, and may include premiums (usually on a monthly basis), enrollment fees, deductibles, copayments, coinsurance, and other similar charges.

CHIP Medicaid Expansions

CHIP Medicaid expansion children must follow the cost-sharing rules of the Medicaid program.60 Under these rules, the majority of such children are exempt from cost sharing.61 However, CHIP Medicaid expansion children may still be subject to service-related cost sharing for non-emergency care provided in an emergency room and for non-preferred prescription drugs. In addition, CHIP Medicaid expansion children enrolled in certain Medicaid waiver programs may be subject to cost sharing.

Separate CHIP Programs

If a state implements a separate CHIP program, premiums or enrollment fees may be imposed for program participation, but the maximum allowable amount is dependent on annual family income.[62] Preventive services and pregnancy-related assistance are exempt from cost sharing for all CHIP families regardless of income, and special rules also apply to Indian children.

- *Families with annual income under 150% FPL*: Premiums may not exceed the amounts set forth in federal Medicaid regulations. Additionally, these families may be charged service-related cost sharing, but such cost sharing is limited to (1) nominal amounts defined in federal Medicaid regulations for the subgroup with annual income below 100% FPL, and (2) slightly higher amounts defined in CHIP regulations for families with annual income between 100%-150% FPL.
- *Families with annual income above 150% FPL*: Cost sharing (program participation fees and service-related cost sharing) may be

> imposed in any amount, provided that cost sharing for higher-income children is not less than cost sharing for lower-income children, subject to the out-of-pocket aggregate limit of 5% of annual family income on all types of cost sharing combined. In addition, states are required to inform families of these limits and provide a mechanism for families to stop paying once the cost-sharing limits have been reached.[63]

The above-referenced study on 42 separate CHIP programs (in 38 states)[64] indicates that only 2 states (Oregon and South Dakota) did not impose any form of cost sharing in 2013. Thirty separate CHIP programs imposed premiums or program participation fees. According to the study, the median monthly premium per child ranged from $10 for families with annual income less than 150% FPL (in 9 programs) to $33 for families with annual income greater than 301% FPL (in 14 programs). Twenty-eight separate CHIP programs imposed service-related cost sharing in amounts that ranged from a low of $0.50 for an office visit or prescription drug in Georgia, to $200.00 for an inpatient hospital visit in Alabama. While Title XXI sets the annual aggregate limit for all cost sharing charges at 5% of a family's annual income, the study found that 20 programs had cost-sharing limits lower than the 5% cap.[65]

CHIP Financing and Expenditures

The federal government and the states jointly finance CHIP.[66] The federal government reimburses states for a portion of every dollar they spend on CHIP (for both CHIP Medicaid expansions and separate CHIP programs) up to state-specific limits called allotments. In FY2013, CHIP expenditures totaled $13.2 billion. The federal share totaled $9.2 billion and the state share was $4.0 billion.[67]

E-FMAP

The federal government pays about 70% of CHIP expenditures, and the federal government's share of CHIP expenditures (including both services and administration) is determined by the enhanced federal medical assistance percentage (E-FMAP) rate. The E-FMAP rate is derived each year by the HHS

Secretary using a set formula, and it varies by state.[68] By statute, the EFMAP (or federal matching rate) can range from 65% to 85%, and in FY2015, the E-FMAP ranges from 65% (13 states) to 82% (Mississippi). See Table A-2 for states' E-FMAP rates for FY2015.

The ACA included a provision to increase the E-FMAP rate by 23 percentage points (not to exceed 100%) for most CHIP expenditures from FY2016 through FY2019. This would increase the statutory range of the E-FMAP rate to 88% through 100%. With this 23 percentage point increase, the federal share of CHIP will be significantly higher, which means states are expected to spend through their limited federal CHIP funding (i.e., state CHIP allotments) faster when the enhanced rate takes effect.

Available Federal Funding

There are three aspects of CHIP federal funding: the national total appropriation amounts, state allotments, and expenditures.

- The federal appropriation is the total amount of federal funds appropriated for CHIP in a fiscal year.
- The state allotments are the federal funds allocated to each state for the federal share of their CHIP expenditures.
- Federal CHIP expenditures are the actual amount of federal funds spent on CHIP.

As Figure 2 shows, in FY2013, the federal appropriation for CHIP was $17.4 billion, the CHIP allotments to states totaled $8.9 billion, and CHIP federal expenditures totaled $9.2 billion. In FY2013, the federal appropriation was significantly higher than the state CHIP allotments because the formula establishing the state CHIP allotment amounts does not factor in the federal appropriation (explained in more detail below). Also, the FY2013 CHIP federal expenditures were slightly higher than the state CHIP allotments. States have two years to spend their allotment funds, and the FY2013 federal CHIP expenditures consist of federal funding from each of the FY2012 and FY2013 state CHIP allotments.

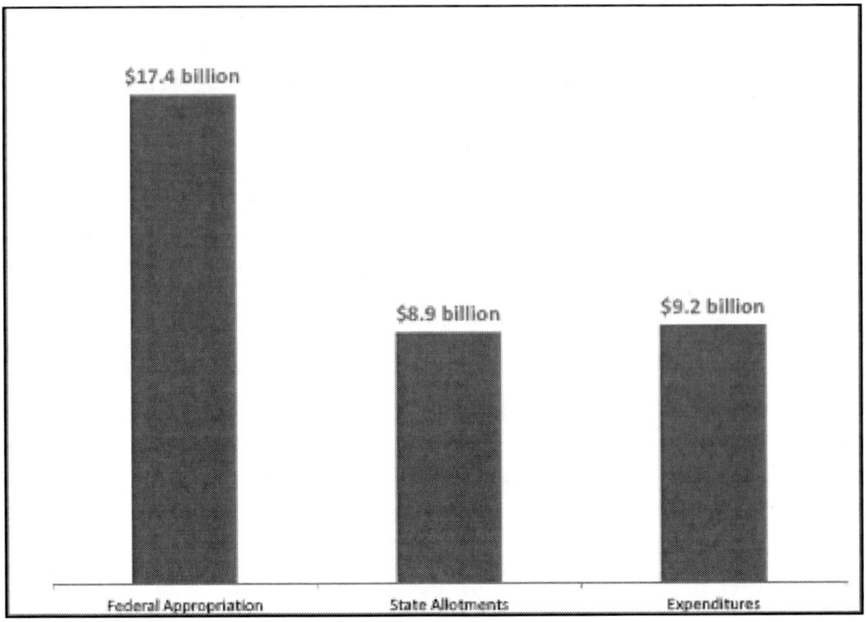

Source: §2104(a)(16) of the Social Security Act; Department of Health and Human Services' Centers for Medicare & Medicaid Services, "Children's Health Insurance Program (CHIP); Final Allotments to States, the District of Columbia, and U.S. Territories and Commonwealths for Fiscal Year 2013," 78 Federal Register 45208, July 26, 2013; Centers for Medicare & Medicaid Services' Office of the Actuary.

Figure 2. Federal Funding for CHIP (FY2013).

Federal Appropriation

The federal appropriation for CHIP is provided in Section 2104(a) of the Social Security Act. This amount is the overall annual ceiling on federal CHIP spending to the states, the District of Columbia, and the territories. CHIPRA increased the annual appropriation amounts substantially beginning in FY2009 and provided appropriations through FY2013. Then, the ACA provided annual appropriation amounts for an additional two years (i.e., through FY2015). MACRA extended the federal appropriations through FY2017, and FY2017 is the last year for which a CHIP appropriation amount is provided. For FY2016 and FY2017, the annual appropriation amounts are $19.3 billion and $20.4 billion,[69] respectively.

If the federal appropriation is not large enough to cover state allotments in any given year, the state allotments would be reduced proportionally. Since

FY2009, the federal appropriation amount has been more than sufficient to cover the state allotments.[70]

State Allotments

State allotments are the federal funds allocated to each state for the federal share of their CHIP expenditures. CHIPRA established a new allocation of federal CHIP funds among the states based largely on states' actual use of and projected need for CHIP funds.[71] There are two formulas for determining state allotments: an even-year formula and an odd-year formula.[72]

In even years, such as FY2014, state CHIP allotments are each state's previous year *allotment* plus any Child Enrollment Contingency Fund (described below) payments from the previous year adjusted for health care inflation and child population growth in the state. For even years, the formula for CHIP allotments can be adjusted to reflect CHIP eligibility or benefit expansions and increase the allotment amount.

In odd years, state CHIP allotments are each state's previous year *spending* (including federal CHIP payments from the state CHIP allotment, Child Enrollment Contingency Fund payments, and redistribution funds) adjusted using the same growth factor as the even year formula (i.e., health care inflation and child population growth in the state). Since the odd-year formula is based on states' actual use of CHIP funds, it is called the "re-basing year" because a state's CHIP allotment can either increase or decrease depending on each state's CHIP expenditures in the previous year.

State CHIP allotment funds are available to states for two years. As noted above, this explains why federal expenditures are higher than the state allotments in Figure 2 because the FY2013 federal CHIP expenditures include federal funding from states' FY2012 and FY2013 allotments. In addition, the aggregate state CHIP allotment amounts have been lower than the annual federal appropriation amount because the allotment formulas do not factor in the annual federal appropriation amount, which means the aggregate state allotment amounts could add up to an amount greater than or less than the federal appropriation amount. Since FY2009, the aggregate state CHIP allotment amounts have been significantly lower than the federal appropriation amount.

The allotment is available to states to cover the federal share of both CHIP benefit and administrative expenditures.[73] However, no more than 10% of the federal CHIP funds that a state draws down from its CHIP allotment can be spent on non-benefit expenditures including expenditures for administration, translation services, and outreach efforts.

Shortfall Funding

If a state's CHIP allotment for the current year, in addition to any allotment funds carried over from the prior year, is insufficient to cover the projected CHIP expenditures for the current year, a few different shortfall funding sources are available. These include Child Enrollment Contingency Fund payments, redistribution funds, and Medicaid funds. Since FY2009, only one state and one territory have received shortfall funding.

Child Enrollment Contingency Fund Payments

Child Enrollment Contingency Fund payments are available to states with both a funding shortfall[74] and CHIP enrollment (for children) that exceeds a target level.[75] As a result, not all states with funding shortfalls are eligible for Child Enrollment Contingency Fund payments.

The contingency fund formula is based on a state's growth in CHIP enrollment and per capita spending. This means that a state may receive a payment from the fund that does not equal its actual shortfall.

Iowa is the only state that has received Child Enrollment Contingency Fund payments since FY2009 when the funds were first available.[76]

Redistribution Funds

After two years, any unused state CHIP allotment funds are redistributed to shortfall states.[77] For redistribution funds, a shortfall state is defined as a state that will not have enough money to meet projected costs in the current year after counting (1) the current year's state allotment, (2) unspent funds from the prior year's state allotment, and (3) available Child Enrollment Contingency Fund payments.

If redistributed funds are insufficient to meet the needs of all shortfall states, each shortfall state receives a proportionate share of the available funds based on the shortfall in each state.

Since FY2009, only Puerto Rico has received redistribution funds.[78]

Medicaid Funds

For states that designed their CHIP program as a CHIP Medicaid expansion or a combination program, if the state is still facing a shortfall after receiving Child Enrollment Contingency Fund payments and redistribution funds, they may receive federal Medicaid matching funds to fund the shortfall in the Medicaid expansion portion of its CHIP program. When Medicaid funds are used to fund CHIP, the state receives the lower regular FMAP rate (i.e., federal Medicaid matching rate) rather than the higher E-FMAP rate provided for other CHIP expenditures. However, while federal CHIP funding is capped, federal Medicaid funding is open-ended, which means there is no upper limit or cap on the amount of federal Medicaid funds a state may receive.

Federal CHIP Funds Finance Some Medicaid Expenditures

In a few situations, federal CHIP funding is used to finance Medicaid expenditures. For instance, certain states significantly expanded Medicaid eligibility for children prior to the enactment of CHIP in 1997.[79] These states are allowed to use their CHIP allotment funds to fund the difference between the Medicaid and CHIP matching rates (i.e., FMAP and E-FMAP rates respectively) to finance the cost for children in Medicaid above 133% FPL.[80]

In addition, states may use CHIP allotment funds and receive the more generous E-FMAP rates for (1) expenditures for children aged 6 to 18 in families with annual income up to 133% FPL that had been enrolled in separate CHIP programs who were transitioned to Medicaid on January 1, 2014, as part of the ACA[81] and (2) children that moved from CHIP to Medicaid due to the application of the 5% income disregard.[82]

CHIP EXPENDITURES

Figure 3 shows actual CHIP expenditures (including both the federal and state share) for FY1998 through FY2013 and projected CHIP expenditures for FY2014 and FY2015. See Table A-2 for CHIP expenditures by state for FY2013.

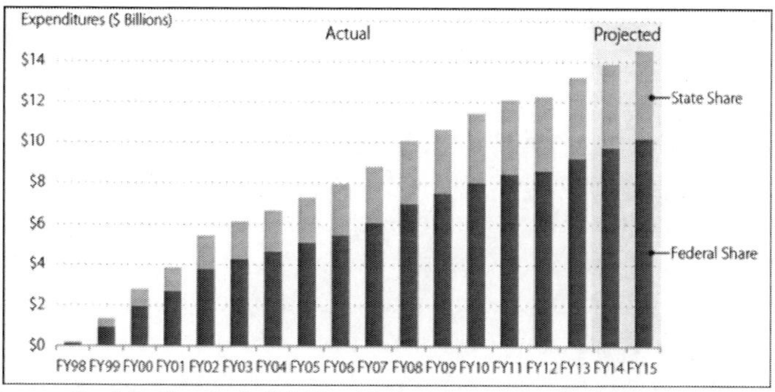

Source: Centers for Medicare & Medicaid Services, Medicaid Financial Management Reports from various years.

Figure 3. CHIP Expenditures, Actual and Projected ($ in billions).

The Future of CHIP

With federal funding for CHIP set to end after FY2017, Congress will need to decide whether to continue the CHIP program. In considering the future of CHIP, it is helpful to recall why the program was created in 1997: to provide affordable health coverage at a time when there were few other insurance coverage options for low-income children outside of Medicaid. The health insurance market is far different today, with the enactment of the ACA. Now, if CHIP funding is exhausted, current CHIP-eligible children potentially could be eligible for Medicaid, for subsidized coverage in the health insurance exchanges, or for their parent's employer-sponsored insurance coverage, but not all CHIP-eligible children would be eligible for these programs and some could end up being uninsured without the availability of CHIP.

Some argue that it is important to continue providing child-specific safety net coverage because each of the low-income subsidy programs (e.g., CHIP, Medicaid, and subsidized exchange coverage) plays a unique role in the health care delivery system.[83] For instance, greater cost-sharing protections exist for the programs that target families at the lower ends of the income-eligibility spectrum.[84] In addition, some are wary of providing coverage for children in the health insurance exchanges because the exchanges are new and there is little evidence about how coverage in the exchanges compares to CHIP coverage.[85]

With FY2017 being the final year for which federal CHIP funding is provided in statute, Congress's action or inaction will determine the future of CHIP and of health coverage for CHIP children. In considering the future of CHIP, Congress has a number of policy options, including extending federal CHIP funding and continuing the program or letting CHIP funding expire.[86]

Extending Federal CHIP Funding

If Congress decides to extend federal CHIP funding, there are a number of policy options to consider, including the length of the funding extension and whether to make programmatic changes. Funding could be extended for just a few years (e.g., two or four years) or indefinitely, and the extension could maintain, phase down, or eliminate the 23 percentage point increase to the E-FMAP rate. In addition, the extension could make programmatic changes to eligibility, benefit coverage, or other aspects of the program.

If Federal CHIP Funding Expires

Although FY2017 is the last year for which federal CHIP funding is provided under current law, states are expected to have federal CHIP spending in FY2018 because states will have access to unspent funds from their FY2017 allotments and to unspent FY2016 allotments redistributed to shortfall states (if any).

If Congress takes no action and CHIP funding runs out, states need to adhere to the MOE requirements that are in effect through FY2019.[87] The MOE requires states to maintain income eligibility levels for CHIP children through September 30, 2019, as a condition for receiving Medicaid payments (notwithstanding the lack of corresponding federal CHIP appropriations for FY2016 through FY2019).[88] The MOE requirements impact CHIP Medicaid expansion programs and separate CHIP programs differently.[89]

- *For CHIP Medicaid expansion programs*, when federal CHIP funding is exhausted, the CHIP-eligible children in these programs continue to be enrolled in Medicaid but financing switches from CHIP to Medicaid.[90] This switch would cause the federal share of expenditures to decrease from the E-FMAP rate to the regular FMAP rate, which means the cost of covering these children would increase for states.
- *For separate CHIP programs*, states are provided a couple of exceptions to the MOE: (1) after September 1, 2015, states may enroll CHIP-eligible children into qualified health plans in the health insurance exchanges[91] or (2) states may impose waiting lists or enrollment caps in order to limit CHIP expenditures. In addition, in the event that a state's CHIP allotment is insufficient to fund CHIP coverage for all eligible children, a state must establish procedures to screen children for Medicaid eligibility, and enroll those who are Medicaid-eligible. For children not eligible for Medicaid, the state must establish procedures to enroll CHIP children in qualified health plans in the health insurance exchanges that have been certified by the HHS Secretary.

If no additional federal CHIP appropriations are provided, CHIP children in CHIP Medicaid expansion programs (roughly half of CHIP enrollees)[92] would continue to receive coverage through the Medicaid program through FY2019,[93] but coverage of CHIP children in separate CHIP programs (roughly half of CHIP enrollees)[94] who are not eligible for Medicaid is reliant on whether the children have access to qualified health plans that are certified by the HHS Secretary. Under the MOE, if states do not receive a CHIP allotment, after establishing procedures to enroll all Medicaid eligible children in Medicaid, states are only required to establish procedures to enroll children in qualified health plans certified by the HHS Secretary. If there are no certified plans, the MOE does not obligate states to provide coverage to these children. If there are certified plans, not all CHIP children will be eligible for subsidized exchange coverage due to the "family glitch,"[95] among other reasons.

Comparing the Coverage Options

Under each of the policy options outlined above under "If Federal CHIP Funding Expires," at least some CHIP enrollees would continue to have coverage through CHIP, Medicaid, the health insurance exchanges, or the employer-sponsored insurance market. However, not all CHIP children would continue to have coverage under each of the policy options.

If the federal CHIP program funding is permitted to expire before (or after) the MOE requirements that are in effect through FY2019, the coverage landscape is expected to change for some portion of the current CHIP enrollees. Although the specific results of coverage projections may look different in future years, it is possible to learn from the information they offer. In anticipation of the FY2015 congressional debate regarding the future of CHIP, the Urban Institute conducted an analysis for MACPAC to generate estimates of the sources of coverage for children in separate CHIP programs who were projected to lose CHIP coverage if federal CHIP funding was exhausted in FY2016.[96] The analysis found that if federal CHIP funding was not renewed and states exhausted their FY2015 federal allotments, approximately two-thirds of current separate CHIP-enrolled children would move to their parent's employer-sponsored insurance coverage (i.e., approximately 1.2 million, or 32.6%) or to subsidized exchange coverage (i.e., approximately 1.4 million, or 36.5%). The remaining one-third of such children (approximately 1.1 million, or 30.9%) would become uninsured in FY2016.[97]

For the children who would receive coverage under alternative coverage options, there would be variation among the coverage in terms of benefits, cost sharing, and financing. With respect to benefit coverage, a recent MACPAC analysis[98] of benefits available under separate CHIP programs, Medicaid, exchange plans, and employer-sponsored insurance found the following:

- Covered benefits vary within each source—between states for Medicaid and CHIP and among plans for exchange plans and employer-sponsored insurance.
- Most CHIP, Medicaid, exchange plans, and employer-sponsored insurance plans cover major medical benefits, such as inpatient and outpatient care, physician services, and prescription drugs.
- Although Medicaid and CHIP cover pediatric dental services, dental benefits are offered as a separate, stand-alone insurance product in most exchanges.
- CHIP and Medicaid cover many services that are not always available in exchange plans. For example, all CHIP and Medicaid programs cover audiology exams, and 95% of CHIP programs cover hearing aids. However, only 37% of exchange plan essential health benefit benchmarks cover audiology exams, and only 54% cover hearing aids.
- For other benefits, such as applied behavioral analysis therapy and autism services, coverage varies.

MACPAC's analysis of affordability of exchange coverage for children currently covered by CHIP found that the out-of-pocket costs for CHIP generally are higher than under Medicaid but significantly lower than in the exchanges or under employer-sponsored insurance.[99] When comparing out-of-pocket costs across coverage types, MACPAC found that for families with employer-sponsored insurance, "projected premiums could average $3,751 per year or 9.1% of family income. Families with subsidized coverage on the exchange might see smaller or no premium costs, but they would face much higher cost-sharing amounts (in the form of deductibles and service-level cost-sharing) than under CHIP."[100]

With respect to financing, under CHIP and Medicaid the coverage for CHIP enrollees would continue to be jointly financed by the federal government and states, but moving CHIP children into Medicaid would increase the state share of expenditures for these children. Under the option to move CHIP children into the health insurance exchanges, the federal government alone would fund the subsidized coverage, without any contribution from states. For employer-sponsored insurance coverage, premiums are largely shared by the employer and its employees.

APPENDIX A. CHIP DATA BY STATE

Table A-1 provides FY2013 data by state regarding CHIP program type, income eligibility levels, and enrollment. Table A-2 shows FY2015 CHIP E-FMAP rates and FY2013 CHIP expenditures (including both federal and state expenditures).

Table A-1. CHIP Program Type, Income Eligibility and Enrollment Information, by State

		FY2013 Program Enrollment[a]			
State and Program Type as of July 1, 2014	Reported Upper Income Level for Children (% FPL)	CHIP Medicaid expansion	Separate CHIP program	Total children enrolled	Pregnant women
Alabama (S*)	317	–	113,490	113,490	–
Alaska (M)	208	16,566	–	16,566	–
Arizona (S*)	205	–	80,238	80,238	–
Arkansas (C)	216	106,413	2,888	109,301	–
California (C)	416	510,424	1,092,859	1,603,283	–
Colorado (C)	265	–	126,169	126,169	4,873
Connecticut (S)	323	–	18,999	18,999	–
Delaware (C)	217	79	13,101	13,180	–
District of Columbia (M)	324	9,057	–	9,057	–
Florida (C)	215	1,072	472,343	473,415	–
Georgia (S*)	252	–	269,906	269,906	–
Hawaii (M)	313	30,979	–	30,979	–
Idaho (C)	190	19,881	25,518	45,399	–
Illinois (C)	318	162,134	174,963	337,097	–
Indiana (C)	255	105,655	46,760	152,415	–
Iowa (C)	380	22,159	61,511	83,670	–
Kansas (S*)	250	–	76,164	76,164	–
Kentucky (C)	218	51,391	32,678	84,069	–
Louisiana (C)	255	140,876	9,092	149,968	–
Maine (C)	213	19,071	10,641	29,712	–
Maryland (M)	322	135,454	–	135,454	–
Massachusetts (C)	305	69,113	79,606	148,719	–
Michigan (C)	217	19,229	70,441	89,670	–

		FY2013 Program Enrollment[a]			
State and Program Type as of July 1, 2014	Reported Upper Income Level for Children (% FPL)	CHIP Medicaid expansion	Separate CHIP program	Total children enrolled	Pregnant women
Minnesota (C)	288	91	3,744	3,835	–
Mississippi (S*)	214	–	93,120	93,120	–
Missouri (C)	305	55,017	37,901	92,918	–
Montana (C)	266	–	31,496	31,496	–
Nebraska (C)	218	53,790	1,993	55,783	–
Nevada (C)	205	–	20,277	20,277	–
New Hampshire (M)	323	19,450	–	19,450	–
New Jersey (C)	355	90,512	116,249	206,761	291
New Mexico (M)	305	9,368	–	9,368	–
New York (C)	405	–	490,114	490,114	–
North Carolina (C)	216	81,656	201,916	283,572	–
North Dakota (C)	175	2,331	8,950	11,281	–
Ohio (M)	211	286,817	–	286,817	–
Oklahoma (C)	210	140,373	7,538	147,911	–
Oregon (S*)	305	–	128,061	128,061	–
Pennsylvania (S*)	319	–	267,073	267,073	–
Rhode Island (C)	266	24,508	2,069	26,577	349
South Carolina (M)	213	76,191	–	76,191	–
South Dakota (C)	209	13,357	4,275	17,632	–
Tennessee (C)	255	22,906	83,567	106,473	–
Texas (S*)	206	–	1,034,613	1,034,613	–
Utah (S*)	205	–	63,001	63,001	–
Vermont (M)	318	–	7,393	7,393	–
Virginia (C)	205	92,690	104,221	196,911	4,636
Washington (S)	305	–	44,073	44,073	–
West Virginia (S*)	305	–	37,065	37,065	–
Wisconsin (C)	306	92,723	74,569	167,292	–
Wyoming (S*)	205	–	8,815	8,815	–
Total		2,481,333	5,649,460	8,130,793	10,149

Source: MACPAC, Report to Congress on Medicaid and CHIP, March 2014, MACSTATS, Tables 3 and 9, and Centers for Medicare & Medicaid Services (CMS), Children's Health Insurance Program Plan Activity, as of July 1, 2014, for information regarding program type.

Notes: State CHIP program type are identified next to the state name with (M) for CHIP Medicaid expansion, (S) for Separate CHIP program, and (C) for a combination of the two approaches. States with (S*) are considered a separate CHIP program by the state, but the CHIP program is technically a combination due to the transition of those aged 6 to 18 up to 133% FPL to Medicaid as required by the ACA.

Enrollment estimates based on ever enrolled data. Enrollment counts reported in the pregnant woman column reflect enrollment estimates associated with states that extend coverage to such individuals through the CHIPRA pregnancy coverage state plan option or through the Section 1115 waiver authority.

State reported Upper Income Level for Children (% FPL) represents the highest income eligibility threshold available in the state either through a CHIP Medicaid expansion, a separate state CHIP, or in combination states—the highest threshold between the two programs. These thresholds have been certified by the Secretary of Health and Human Services (HHS) as representing the conversion from the state's old income counting rules to the new income counting rules based on MAGI and include the 5% disregard (which the law provides as a standard disregard).

FPL: Federal poverty level.

[a] In FY2013, there were 219,473 adults enrolled in the CHIP program. CHIPRA terminated CHIP coverage of nonpregnant childless adults by the end of calendar year 2009, prohibited new states from obtaining waivers to extend CHIP coverage to uninsured parents, and phased out coverage of parents altogether by FY2014. Source: MACPAC, Report to Congress on Medicaid and CHIP, March 2014, MACSTATS, Table 3.

Table A-2. E-FMAP Rates and CHIP Expenditures by State

		FY2013 CHIP Expenditures ($ in millions)		
State	FY2015 E-FMAP	Total	Federal	State
Alabama	78.29%	$193.4	$150.8	$42.6
Alaska	65.00	32.8	21.3	11.5
Arizona	77.92	73.9	56.1	17.7
Arkansas	79.62	122.8	95.4	27.4
California	65.00	2,126.8	1,382.4	744.4
Colorado	65.71	227.3	147.7	79.5
Connecticut	65.00	28.0	18.2	9.8
Delaware	67.54	24.6	17.0	7.6
District of Columbia	79.00	18.4	14.5	3.9
Florida	71.80	520.7	367.5	153.2
Georgia	76.86	413.3	313.6	99.7

		FY2013 CHIP Expenditures ($ in millions)		
State	FY2015 E-FMAP	Total	Federal	State
Hawaii	66.56	40.3	26.6	13.7
Idaho	80.23	60.7	48.3	12.4
Illinois	65.53	517.7	336.4	181.3
Indiana	76.56	157.4	121.2	36.2
Iowa	68.88	134.2	96.2	38.0
Kansas	69.64	75.5	52.5	23.0
Kentucky	78.96	184.8	146.7	38.1
Louisiana	73.44	203.3	148.1	55.2
Maine	73.32	37.2	27.5	9.7
Maryland	65.00	258.4	168.0	90.4
Massachusetts	65.00	573.7	372.9	200.8
Michigan	75.88	147.1	112.5	34.7
Minnesota	65.00	19.5	12.8	6.7
Mississippi	81.51	207.5	168.9	38.6
Missouri	74.42	170.0	124.1	45.8
Montana	76.13	91.5	69.7	21.8
Nebraska	67.29	70.1	48.2	21.9
Nevada	75.05	37.2	26.8	10.5
New Hampshire	65.00	16.7	10.9	5.9
New Jersey	65.00	958.0	586.6	371.5
New Mexico	78.76	144.9	110.0	35.0
New York	65.00	959.9	624.0	335.9
North Carolina	76.12	398.0	302.0	96.1
North Dakota	65.00	26.6	17.7	8.9
Ohio	73.85	381.3	284.1	97.2
Oklahoma	73.61	172.6	129.1	43.5
Oregon	74.84	209.4	154.3	55.0
Pennsylvania	66.27	428.0	291.1	136.9
Rhode Island	65.00	81.1	53.7	27.4
South Carolina	79.45	132.5	105.1	27.4
South Dakota	66.15	24.6	17.0	7.6
Tennessee	75.49	259.6	198.0	61.6
Texas	70.64	1,285.0	918.8	366.2
Utah	79.39	68.6	54.0	14.6
Vermont	67.81	9.0	6.2	2.8
Virginia	65.00	301.0	195.7	105.4
Washington	65.02	122.9	79.9	42.9
West Virginia	79.95	57.9	46.5	11.3
Wisconsin	70.79	140.3	100.7	39.6
Wyoming	65.00	16.4	10.7	5.7

Table A-2. (Continued)

		FY2013 CHIP Expenditures ($ in millions)		
State	FY2015 E-FMAP	Total	Federal	State
Total		$12,962.4	$8,987.9	$3,974.5

Source: Department of Health and Human Services, "Federal Financial Participation in State Assistance Expenditures; Federal Matching Shares for Medicaid, the Children's Health Insurance Program, and Aid to Needy Aged, Blind, or Disabled Persons for October 1, 2014 Through September 30, 2015," 79 Federal Register 3385, January 21, 2014; U.S. Department of Health and Human Services, Centers for Medicare and Medicaid Services, Form CMS-64 data.

Notes: This table does not include CHIP expenditures in the territories or CHIP expenditures under §2105(g) of the Social Security Act, which permits 11 qualifying states to use CHIP funds to pay the difference between the FMAP rate (i.e., the federal Medicaid matching rate) and the E-FMAP rate for Medicaid-enrolled, Medicaid-financed children whose family annual income exceed 133% FPL. These are CHIP funds used to finance children in Medicaid, and states are not required to match the federal funds provided in §2105(g) of the Social Security Act.

Appendix B. Upper Income Eligibility Levels in Medicaid, CHIP, and Subsidized Exchange Coverage

State-by-state income eligibility level for Medicaid, CHIP, and subsidized exchange coverage for infants, children aged 1 to 5, children aged 6 to 18, and pregnant women and unborn children are provided in Figure B-1, Figure B-2, Figure B-3, and Figure B-4 (respectively).

Most children and pregnant women in families with income under 400% of the federal poverty level (FPL) are eligible for Medicaid, CHIP, or subsidized exchange coverage. The income eligibility levels for Medicaid and CHIP vary by state and population (i.e., age of child or pregnant women), and subsidized exchange coverage[101] is available for most children and pregnant women with incomes between 100% FPL and 400% FPL that do not have access to other minimum essential coverage,[102] such as Medicaid or CHIP.

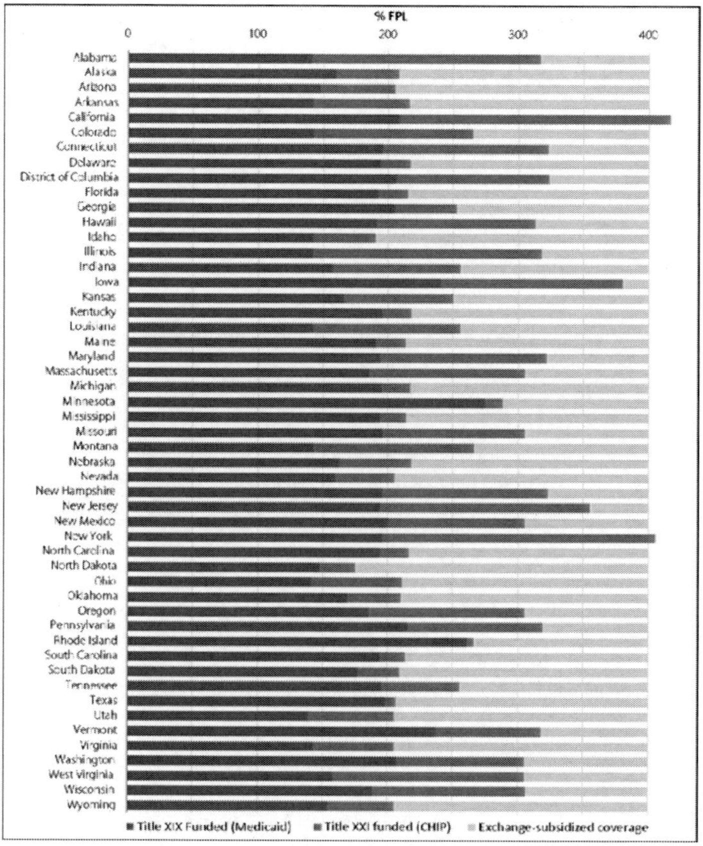

Source: MACPAC, Report to Congress on Medicaid and CHIP, March 2014, MACStats, Table 9.

Notes: Upper income levels (% FPL) represent the highest income eligibility threshold available in the state, and include the 5% disregard (which the law provides as a standard disregard).

It is important to note that CHIP coverage is limited to uninsured children, so children who have health insurance coverage and fall in the income eligibility range shown for CHIP are nonetheless not CHIP eligible because of their insurance status.

In one county in California and New York, CHIP coverage for CHIP children extends to a higher income eligibility threshold than subsidized exchange coverage (i.e., 416% FPL in one county and 405% FPL, respectively). Email correspondence with CMS from March 9, 2015, indicates that California's CHIP expansion to 416% FPL was approved by CMS but never implemented by the state.

FPL: Federal poverty level.

Figure B-1. Upper Income Eligibility Levels for Infants, as a Percentage of the FPL in Medicaid, CHIP, and Subsidized Exchange Coverage by State (as of January 1, 2014).

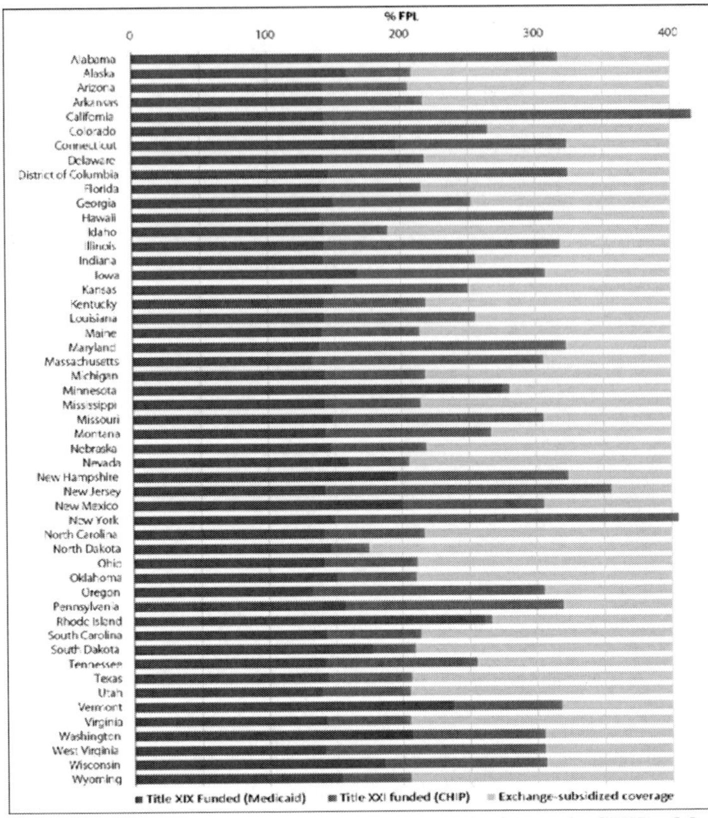

Source: MACPAC, Report to Congress on Medicaid and CHIP, March 2014, MACStats, Table 9.

Notes: Upper income levels (% FPL) represent the highest income eligibility threshold available in the state, and include the 5% disregard (which the law provides as a standard disregard).

It is important to note that CHIP coverage is limited to uninsured children, so children who have health insurance coverage and fall in the income eligibility range shown for CHIP are nonetheless not CHIP eligible because of their insurance status.

In one county in California and New York, CHIP coverage for CHIP children extends to a higher income eligibility threshold than subsidized exchange coverage (i.e., 416% FPL in one county and 405% FPL, respectively). Email correspondence with CMS from March 9, 2015, indicates that California's CHIP expansion to 416% FPL was approved by CMS but never implemented by the state.

FPL: Federal poverty level.

Figure B-2. Upper Income Eligibility Levels for Children Aged 1 Through 5, as a Percentage of the FPL in Medicaid, CHIP, and Subsidized Exchange Coverage by State (as of January 1, 2014).

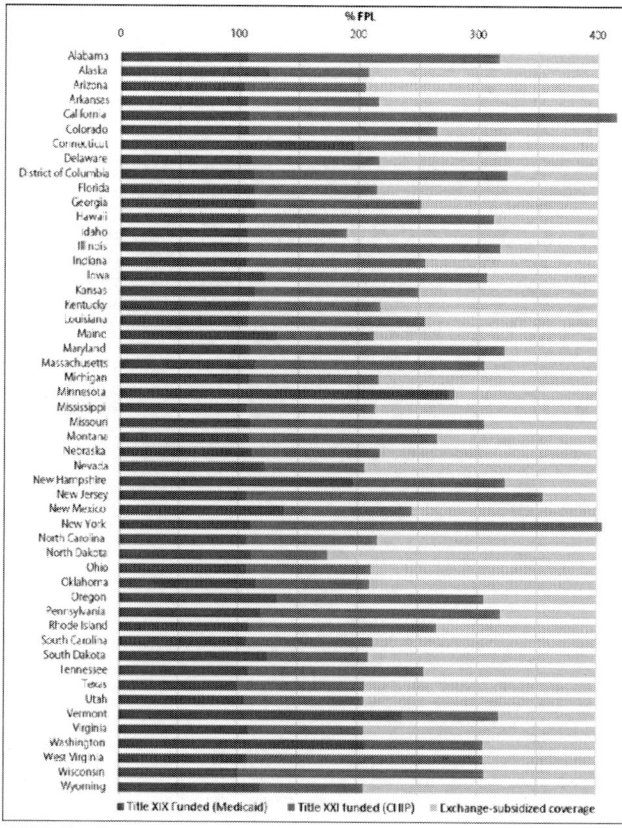

Source: MACPAC, Report to Congress on Medicaid and CHIP, March 2014, MACStats, Table 9.

Notes: Upper income levels (% FPL) represent the highest income eligibility threshold available in the state, and include the 5% disregard (which the law provides as a standard disregard).

It is important to note that CHIP coverage is limited to uninsured children, so children who have health insurance coverage and fall in the income eligibility range shown for CHIP are nonetheless not CHIP eligible because of their insurance status.

In one county in California and New York, CHIP coverage for CHIP children extends to a higher income eligibility threshold than subsidized exchange coverage (i.e., 416% FPL in one county and 405% FPL, respectively). Email correspondence with CMS from March 9, 2015, indicates that California's CHIP expansion to 416% FPL was approved by CMS but never implemented by the state.

FPL: Federal poverty level.

Figure B-3. Upper Income Eligibility Levels for Children Aged 6 Through 18, as a Percentage of the FPL in Medicaid, CHIP, and Subsidized Exchange Coverage by State (as of January 1, 2014).

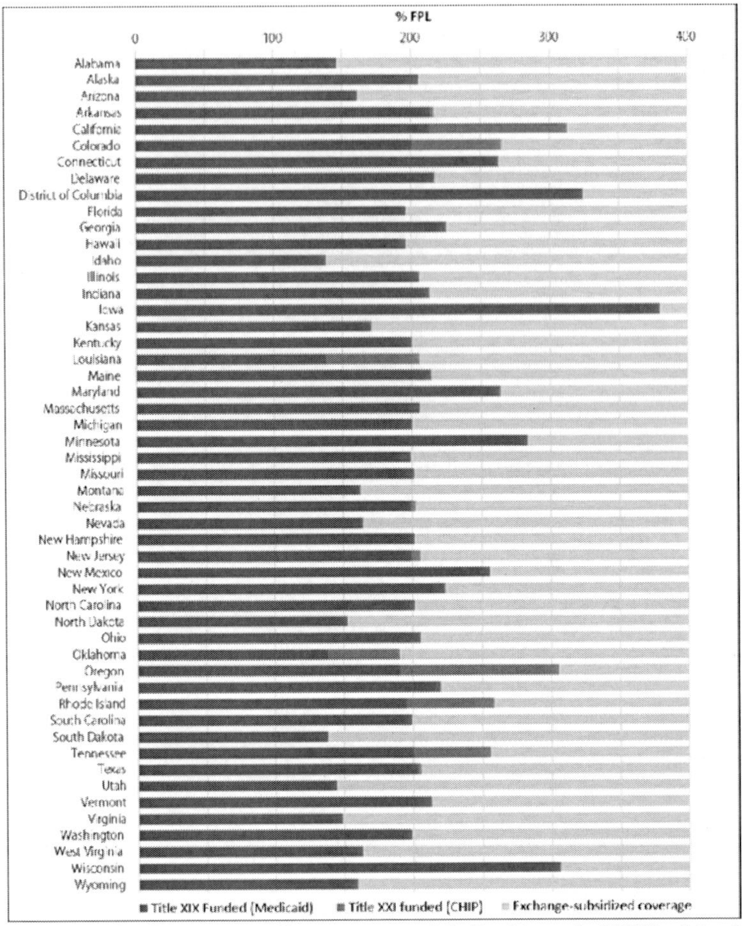

Source: MACPAC, Report to Congress on Medicaid and CHIP, March 2014, MACStats, Table 9.

Notes: Upper income levels (% FPL) represent the highest income eligibility threshold available in the state, and include the 5% disregard (which the law provides as a standard disregard).

As of January 2014, 15 states extended CHIP coverage to unborn children in Arkansas, California, Illinois, Louisiana, Massachusetts, Michigan, Minnesota, Nebraska, Oklahoma, Oregon, Rhode Island, Tennessee, Texas, Washington and Wisconsin. State income eligibility boundaries associated with the unborn child pathway are not shown here.

FPL: Federal poverty level.

Figure B-4. Upper Income Eligibility Levels for Pregnant Women and Unborn Children, as a Percentage of the FPL in Medicaid, CHIP, and Subsidized Exchange Coverage by State (as of January 1, 2014).

End Notes

[1] The five territories are American Samoa, Guam, the Commonwealth of the Northern Mariana Islands, Puerto Rico, and the Virgin Islands.

[2] For more information on the changes enacted under the Children's Health Insurance Program Reauthorization Act of 2009 (CHIPRA; P.L. 111-3), see CRS Report R40226, P.L. 111-3: The Children's Health Insurance Program Reauthorization Act of 2009, by Evelyne P. Baumrucker, Elicia J. Herz, and Jane G. Gravelle.

[3] For more information about the changes enacted under the Patient Protection and Affordable Care Act (ACA; P.L. 111-148, as amended), see CRS Report R41210, Medicaid and the State Children's Health Insurance Program (CHIP) Provisions in ACA: Summary and Timeline, by Evelyne P. Baumrucker et al.

[4] For more information on the provisions included in the Medicare Access and CHIP Reauthorization Act of 2015 (MACRA; P.L. 114-10), see CRS Report R43962, H.R. 2: The Medicare Access and CHIP Reauthorization Act of 2015, coordinated by Jim Hahn and Kirstin B. Blom.

[5] For more information about Medicaid, see CRS Report R43357, Medicaid: An Overview, coordinated by Alison Mitchell.

[6] CHIP Medicaid expansions are not impacted by the ACA Medicaid expansion, under which states have the option to extend Medicaid coverage to most nonelderly, nonpregnant adults with income up to 133% of the federal poverty level (FPL). For more information about the ACA Medicaid expansion, see CRS Report R43564, The ACA Medicaid Expansion, by Alison Mitchell.

[7] For example, the state of Florida's CHIP combination program includes a CHIP Medicaid expansion (i.e., Medicaid), and three separate CHIP programs (i.e., MediKids, Healthy Kids, and the Children's Medical Services Network).

[8] States decide on CHIP program design based on a variety of factors including willingness to expand an individual entitlement in the state, desire to offer a program that looks more like private health insurance coverage, etc.

[9] Administrative data permits the federal government and states to track CHIP program enrollment and spending. States use the Statistical Enrollment Data System (SEDS) to report aggregate CHIP and Medicaid child enrollment by program type (Medicaid, CHIP Medicaid expansion, and separate CHIP program), age, gender, and race/ethnicity, among other criteria. States report actual expenditures for Medicaid and CHIP Medicaid expansion programs on the Form CMS 64. Actual expenditures for separate CHIP programs are reported on the Form CMS-37.

[10] Under §1115 of the Social Security Act, the Secretary of Health and Human Services (HHS) may waive CHIP program requirements so states can test new program design options that further the goals of the CHIP program. CHIP 1115 waivers are time limited (up to five years) and must be allotment-neutral to the federal government. In other words, they cannot cost the federal government more than what is available under the state's annual allotment(s) applicable to the fiscal years for which the demonstration is operational. For a list of states with operational CHIP Section 1115 waiver programs, see http://www.medicaid.gov/Medicaid-CHIP-Program-Information/By-Topics/ Waivers/Waivers.html.

[11] As of July 1, 2014, 2 states (Washington and Connecticut) had separate CHIP programs with no Medicaid expansions. The remaining 11 states (Alabama, Arizona, Georgia, Kansas, Oregon, Mississippi, Pennsylvania, Texas, Utah, West Virginia, and Wyoming) are

considered to have separate CHIP programs, but technically these programs are part of combination CHIP programs due to the ACA requirement to transition CHIP children aged 6 through 18 in families with annual income less than 133% of the federal poverty level (based on modified adjusted gross income, or MAGI) to Medicaid, beginning January 1, 2014.

[12] Centers for Medicare & Medicaid Services (CMS), Children's Health Insurance Program Plan Activity, as of July 1, 2014.

[13] Medicaid and CHIP Payment and Access Commission (MACPAC), Report to the Congress on Medicaid and CHIP, March 2014.

[14] MACPAC, Report to the Congress on Medicaid and CHIP, March 2015.

[15] States are permitted to require a period of uninsurance (i.e., waiting period) of up to 90 days before a child who is otherwise eligible is permitted to enroll in CHIP. See 78 Federal Register 42160, July 15, 2013.

[16] §2110(b) of the Social Security Act.

[17] In the early years of the CHIP program, states were permitted and encouraged to extend coverage to uninsured pregnant women, parents, and childless adults age 19 and over generally through the use of the Section 1115 waiver authority. However, Congress acted to largely limit this practice through a series of laws. The Deficit Reduction Act of 2005 (P.L. 109-171) prohibited the use of CHIP funds from coverage of non-pregnant childless adults in any new waivers approved after February 8, 2006. CHIPRA terminated CHIP coverage of nonpregnant childless adults by the end of calendar year 2009, prohibited new states from obtaining waivers to extend CHIP coverage to uninsured parents, and phased out coverage of parents altogether by FY2014. States can still extend coverage to adult pregnant women (regardless of their age) under CHIP through a variety of mechanisms. For more information on the predominate pathways states use to extend CHIP coverage to pregnant woman, see the Eligibility subsection entitled, "Pregnant Women and Unborn Children."

[18] Federal Medicaid statute establishes mandatory coverage floors (defined as a percentage of the federal poverty level) for its poverty-related pregnant women and children eligibility groups. States are permitted to extend coverage above these federal minimum thresholds which is why there is variability across states in terms of the income eligibility threshold at which CHIP begins.

[19] Because individuals can have other health insurance and still be covered by Medicaid, this approach also allows states to bring into Medicaid otherwise ineligible higher-income children regardless of their other health insurance status. For example, under this strategy, states can provide Medicaid benefits to additional children for whom existing health insurance is limited (sometimes referred to as under-insured). When states liberalize the financial rules for existing Medicaid eligibility groups, the federal share of the costs for services provided to the subset without other health insurance—the CHIP-eligible children—is paid for out of CHIP funds. The federal share of the costs for services delivered to the remaining children with other health insurance is paid for by Medicaid. CHIP Medicaid expansion children represent an optional eligibility pathway under Medicaid.

[20] §2102(b) of the Social Security Act.

[21] States are permitted to offer different benefit packages for children with special needs, as long as the eligibility criteria for that coverage comply with the Americans with Disabilities Act (ADA) requirements for non-discrimination. Source: The Administration's Responses to Questions About the State Children's Health Insurance Program, July 29, 1998, Fifth Set.

[22] A CHIP child must not be found eligible for Medicaid, or other group health coverage, for example. See 42 C.F.R. §457.310.

[23] States are permitted to continue coverage for CHIP-eligible children for a period of 12 months regardless of changes in family composition or income that may otherwise affect their eligibility status. While no explicit statutory authority for 12 months of continuous coverage currently exists in CHIP statute, HHS reports that 33 states provided 12 months of continuous coverage to CHIP children in FY2012. Source: MACPAC, Report to the Congress on Medicaid and CHIP, March 2013.

[24] Income disregards (including block of income disregards) and deductions effectively increase the amount of income a child's family can have and still be eligible for coverage, as they serve to eliminate from a family's countable income certain expenses, costs or amounts of income.

[25] Medicaid and CHIP financial eligibility requirements place limits on the maximum amount of income (and sometimes assets) individuals may possess to become eligible (often referred to as standards or thresholds). Additional guidelines specify how states should calculate these amounts (i.e., counting methodologies).

[26] Under CHIPRA, new states (in addition to California, New Jersey, and New York) were discouraged from expanding CHIP income eligibility through a policy that required a reduction in federal CHIP payments for coverage of children in families with income above 300% FPL. CHIPRA also included other provisions to provide financial incentives to states to find and enroll Medicaid eligible children at lower income levels through the use of CHIP Performance Bonus Payments. These payments were directed at states that adopted 5 out of 8 enrollment facilitation strategies and that successfully enrolled Medicaid-eligible children over target enrollment levels. These bonus payments expired at the end of FY2013.

[27] MAGI is defined as the Internal Revenue Code's (IRC's) adjusted gross income (AGI) plus certain foreign earned income and tax-exempt interest. AGI reflects a number of deductions, including trade and business deductions, losses from sale of property, and alimony payments, increased by tax-exempt interest and income earned by U.S. citizens or residents living abroad.

[28] §2102(b)(1)(B)(v) of the Social Security Act.

[29] Under the ACA, certain groups are exempt from income eligibility determinations for Medicaid based on MAGI. Prior law's income determination rules will continue to be used for determining eligibility for the following groups: (1) individuals who are eligible for Medicaid through another federal or state assistance program (e.g., foster care children and individuals receiving SSI), (2) the elderly, (3) certain disabled individuals who qualify for Medicaid on the basis of being blind or disabled without regard to whether the individual is eligible for SSI, (4) the medically needy, and (5) enrollees in a Medicare Savings Program (e.g., Qualified Medicare Beneficiaries for whom Medicaid pays Medicare premiums or coinsurance and deductibles). In addition, MAGI does not affect eligibility determinations through Express Lane enrollment (to determine whether a child has met Medicaid or CHIP eligibility requirements), for Medicare prescription drug low-income subsidies, or for determinations of eligibility for Medicaid long-term services and supports.

[30] Under the transition to MAGI, states were given a limited opportunity to expand CHIP eligibility above 200% of the FPL (not to exceed 300% FPL) using the old income counting rules by submitting a state plan amendment (SPA) before December 31, 2013.

[31] States must provide coverage through a separate CHIP program to children who lose Medicaid as a result of the elimination of income disregards permitted under §2101(f) of the ACA. Coverage for this population will be paid for out of the state's CHIP allotment at the CHIP

enhanced match rate and will cease when the last child protected has been afforded 12 months of coverage (expected to be no later than April 1, 2016). While coverage of children protected by 2101(f) is mandated through a separate CHIP program, states may instead continue to provide coverage of these children in the state's Medicaid program. However, if a state chooses the option to maintain Medicaid eligibility for such children, funds through Title XIX of SSA and regular FMAP rates will apply. Sources: Centers for Medicare and Medicaid Services, Medicaid/CHIP Affordable Care Act Implementation: Children's Health Insurance Program (CHIP) coverage for children who lose Medicaid eligibility due to the elimination of income disregards as a result of the conversion to MAGI. Section 2101(f) of the Affordable Care Act: Answers to Frequently Asked Questions; April 25, 2013; and CMS Answers to Frequently Asked Questions: Telephonic Applications, Medicaid and CHIP Eligibility Policy and 75/25 Federal Matching Rate, August 9, 2013.

[32] Coverage for such children will continue to be paid for out of the state's CHIP annual allotment at the enhanced CHIP matching rate. CMS granted approval for Pennsylvania to delay the transition of CHIP children in families with income less than 133% FPL based on MAGI until FY2015.

[33] Vernon K. Smith, Kathleen Gifford, and Eileen Ellis, Health Management Associates and Robin Rudowitz and Laura Snyder, Kaiser Family Foundation, Medicaid in an Era of Health and Delivery System Reform: Results from a 50-State Medicaid Budget Survey for State Fiscal Years 2014 and 2015, October 2014.

[34] Kaiser Family Foundation, Kaiser Commission on Medicaid and the Uninsured, Aligning Eligibility For Children: Moving the Stairstep Kids to Medicaid, August 2013.

[35] Specifically, with the exception of waiting lists for enrolling children in CHIP or enrolling CHIP-eligible children in certified exchange plans when federal CHIP funding is no longer available, states cannot implement eligibility standards, methodologies, or procedures that are more restrictive than those in place on March 31, 2010. §2105(d)(3) of the Social Security Act.

[36] Most counties in California are in the state's CHIP Medicaid expansion program, which extends coverage up to 266% FPL. However, the state had a separate CHIP program that extended CHIP coverage up to 321% FPL in three counties, and up to 416% FPL in one county (Email correspondence with CMS from March 9, 2015 indicates that California's CHIP expansion to 416% FPL in one county was approved by CMS, but never implemented by the state). During FY2013, children in the state's separate CHIP program were transitioned to the state's CHIP Medicaid expansion program.

[37] Federal authority for Arizona's CHIP program to cover children in families with annual income above 100% FPL expired on January 31, 2014. As a result, children in families with income between 100-133% FPL transitioned to Medicaid effective January 1, 2014. Children in families with income over 133% FPL were encouraged to apply for coverage through the health insurance exchange where premium subsidies are available for eligible households. While the state's CHIP program to extend coverage for CHIP-eligible children in families with annual income less than 100% FPL remains in effect, enrollment of new children has been frozen since January 1, 2010. As a result of the enrollment freeze, enrollment in Arizona's CHIP program has dropped from 45.8 thousand in January 2010 to approximately 2.3 thousand in February 2014. Source: Tricia Brooks, Martha Heberlein, and Joseph Fu, Georgetown University Health Policy Institute, Center for Children and Families, Dismantling CHIP in Arizona: How Losing KidsCare Impacts a Child's Health Care Costs, May 2014.

[38] For more information on the access to private insurance coverage among low-income children in CHIP, see Mathematica Policy Research, CHIPRA Mandated Evaluation of the Children's Health Insurance Program: Final Findings, August 1, 2014.

[39] Email correspondence with CMS from March 9, 2015, indicates that California's CHIP expansion to 416% FPL in one county was approved by CMS but never implemented by the state.

[40] The definition of minimum essential coverage is broad. It includes Medicare Part A, Medicaid, the State Children's Health Insurance Program (CHIP), Tricare, the TRICARE for Life program, the veteran's health care program, the Peace Corps program, a government plan (local, state, federal) including the Federal Employees Health Benefits Program (FEHBP) and any plan established by an Indian tribal government, any plan offered in the individual, small group or large group market, a grandfathered health plan, and any other health benefits coverage, such as a state health benefits risk pool, as recognized by the HHS Secretary in coordination with the Treasury Secretary.

[41] The enrollment figures reported here represent "ever enrolled" counts which measure the number of children covered by CHIP or Medicaid for any period of time during a given year. These enrollment counts differ significantly from estimates based on "point-in-time" or average annual enrollment measures. Source: MACPAC Report to Congress on Medicaid and CHIP, March 2014, Table 4.

[42] For example, it is possible that a state with a large uninsured child population but a CHIP program with a relatively narrow income eligibility range may result in a much larger number of CHIP program enrollees than a state with a relatively small uninsured child population and a CHIP program with a much broader income eligibility range. For example, in Texas, the CHIP eligibility range appears small by comparison with the CHIP eligibility range in Louisiana (See Figure B-1, Figure B-2, and Figure B-3). However, in FY2013, CMS administrative data show CHIP child enrollment totaling approximately 1 million in Texas as compared with approximately 150,000 in Louisiana (See Table A-1).

[43] Prior to the enactment of CHIPRA, legal immigrants arriving in the United States after August 22, 1996, were ineligible for Medicaid or CHIP benefits for their first five years in the United States. With the enactment of CHIPRA, states are permitted to provide Medicaid and/or CHIP coverage to children under the age of 21 and pregnant women who are (1) lawfully residing in the United States and (2) otherwise eligible for such coverage. The CHIP state plan option is available to states that (1) elect this state plan option under Medicaid and (2) in the case of lawfully residing pregnant women, elect the CHIP state plan option to provide assistance for pregnant women. As of March 24, 2014, 28 states and the District of Columbia extend Medicaid and/or CHIP coverage to lawfully residing children, and 23 states and the District of Columbia extend Medicaid and/or CHIP coverage to lawfully residing pregnant women. See CMS, Medicaid and CHIP Coverage of Lawfully Residing Children and Pregnant Women, at http://www.medicaid.gov/ medicaid-chip-program-information/by-topics/outreach-and-enrollment/lawfully-residing.html.

[44] MACPAC, Report to Congress on Medicaid and CHIP, March 2014, Table 9, pp 80-82.

[45] States that wish to make changes to their Medicaid or CHIP state plans must submit a state plan amendment (SPA) to CMS for approval.

[46] MACPAC, Report to Congress on Medicaid and CHIP, March 2014, Table 9, pp 80-82.

[47] Medicaid's mandatory and optional benefits are identified in federal statute and regulations, and include a wide range of preventive, primary, and acute medical services, as well as long-term services and supports (LTSS). States define the specific features of each covered benefit within broad federal guidelines.

[48] The ACA requires Medicaid ABP coverage to include the same essential health benefits (EHBs) provided in exchange plans. For more information about Medicaid benefit coverage, see CRS Report R43357, Medicaid: An Overview, coordinated by Alison Mitchell.

[49] §2103 of the Social Security Act.

[50] §2103 of the Social Security Act.

[51] Actuarial value is a summary measure of a plan's generosity, expressed as a percentage of medical expenses estimated to be paid by the issuer for a standard population and set of allowed charges.

[52] Three states, Florida, New York and Pennsylvania were permitted to use the state's health coverage plan that was in place at the time of CHIP's enactment. These benefit packages are often referred to as "grandfathered plans."

[53] Dental services were added as a required benefit for separate CHIP programs under CHIPRA, and include services necessary to prevent disease and promote oral health, restore oral structures to health and function, and treat emergency conditions. (Dental benefits have always been required for CHIP Medicaid expansion children via EPSDT.)

[54] In the case of a state separate CHIP program that provides medical and surgical benefits as well as mental health or substance abuse disorder benefits, the predominant financial requirements (e.g., deductibles, copayments) and treatment limitations (e.g., number of visits, days of coverage) applicable to such mental health or substance abuse disorder benefits must be no more restrictive than the predominant financial requirements and treatment limitations applicable to covered medical and surgical benefits. In addition, there can be no separate cost-sharing requirements or treatment limitations applicable only to mental health or substance abuse disorder benefits. State CHIP Medicaid expansions that include coverage of EPSDT services (as defined in Medicaid statute) are deemed to satisfy these mental health parity requirements. For more information, see CMS Letter to Medicaid Directors and State Health Officials, RE: Application of the Mental Health Parity and Addiction Equity Act to Medicaid MCOs, CHIP, and Alternative Benefit (Benchmark) Plans, SHO # 13-001, ACA #24, January 16, 2013, available at http://www.medicaid.gov/Federal-Policy-Guidance/downloads/SHO-13-001.pdf.

[55] Historically, it has proved prohibitive for many employer plans and states to meet all of these requirements. To circumvent these restrictions, most states operating CHIP or Medicaid premium assistance programs do so under Section 1115 waiver authority.

[56] Anita Cardwell, et al., National Academy for State Health Policy and Georgetown University Health Policy Institute, Center for Children and Families; Benefits and Cost Sharing in Separate CHIP Programs, May 2014.

[57] For example, of the 25 states with Secretary approved coverage, 14 states modeled their coverage after the state's Medicaid program, and 11 of these 14 states offered EPSDT as a part of the state's separate CHIP program benefits.

[58] Anita Cardwell, et al., National Academy for State Health Policy and Georgetown University Health Policy Institute, Center for Children and Families; Benefits and Cost Sharing in Separate CHIP Programs, May 2014.

[59] MACPAC, Report to Congress on Medicaid and CHIP, March 2014.

[60] §1916 of the Social Security Act.

[61] For more information about Medicaid cost sharing rules, see CRS Report R43357, Medicaid: An Overview, coordinated by Alison Mitchell. An exception to this rule applies for CHIP-eligible pregnant women and infants with annual income greater than 150% FPL. Such individuals may be charged premiums or enrollment fees in "nominal" amounts. Nominal

amounts are set in regulation and range from $1 to $20 per month, depending on monthly family income and family size. States are permitted to charge premiums/enrollment fees that exceed these nominal amounts for certain groups, including CHIP-eligible pregnant women.

[62] §2103(e) of the Social Security Act.

[63] CHIP cost-sharing limits do not take into account cumulative out-of-pocket costs that may be required for "split families" for whom, in addition to CHIP, one or more family member(s) may be eligible for subsidized exchange coverage, and/or enrolled in Medicaid and are simultaneously subject to the cost sharing requirements associated with each program. This issue is often referred to as "premium stacking."

[64] Anita Cardwell, Joanne Jee, and Catherine Hess, National Academy for State Health Policy and Joe Touschner, Martha Heberlein, and Joan Alker, Georgetown University Center for Children and Families; Benefits and Cost Sharing in Separate CHIP Programs, May 2014.

[65] For more recent information on state changes to cost sharing requirements under Medicaid and CHIP, see Vernon K. Smith, Kathleen Gifford, and Eileen Ellis, Health Management Associates and Robin Rudowitz and Laura Snyder, Kaiser Family Foundation, Medicaid in an Era of Health and Delivery System Reform: Results from a 50-State Medicaid Budget Survey for State Fiscal Years 2014 and 2015, October 2014. This information has not been summarized here.

[66] For more information about federal CHIP financing, see CRS Report R43949, Federal Financing for the State Children's Health Insurance Program (CHIP), by Alison Mitchell.

[67] U.S. Department of Health and Human Services, Centers for Medicare and Medicaid Services, Form CMS-64 data.

[68] The E-FMAP is calculated by reducing the state share under the FMAP rate (which is the federal matching rate for most Medicaid expenditures) by 30%. For more information about the FMAP rate and how it is calculated, see CRS Report R43847, Medicaid's Federal Medical Assistance Percentage (FMAP), FY2016, by Alison Mitchell.

[69] The FY2017 appropriation is the combination of two half-year appropriations of $2.85 billion from §2104(a) of the Social Security Act plus a one-time appropriation in the amount of $14.70 billion from §301(b)(3) of MACRA.

[70] From FY2002 through FY2008, the federal appropriation amounts were insufficient to cover the full cost of some states' CHIP programs. For FY2002 through FY2005, the amount of redistribution funds from other states was enough to make up the difference, but for FY2006 through FY2008, additional CHIP appropriations were provided to cover the cost of the federal share of CHIP expenditures.

[71] Prior to CHIPRA, funds were allocated to states using a statutory formula based on each state's share of the nation's uninsured children and uninsured low-income children.

[72] §2104(m) of the Social Security Act.

[73] CHIP Medicaid expansion states may use federal Medicaid funds to pay for CHIP administrative expenditures.

[74] For Child Enrollment Contingency Fund payments, a state has a funding shortfall if a state's current year CHIP allotment plus any unused CHIP allotment funds from the previous year are insufficient to cover the federal share of the state's CHIP program. The definition of shortfall funding for Child Enrollment Contingency Fund payments does not factor in redistribution funds.

[75] §2104(n) of the Social Security Act.

[76] In FY2011, Iowa had a projected shortfall in federal CHIP funding of $3.8 million. Since Iowa's CHIP enrollment exceeded the target level, Iowa was eligible for a Child Enrollment

Contingency Fund payment and received $28.9 million. (MACPAC, MAC Basics: Federal CHIP Financing, September 2011; Communication with the Centers for Medicare & Medicaid Services in May 2014.)

[77] §2104(f) of the Social Security Act.

[78] In FY2012 and FY2013, Puerto Rico received $23.7 million and $0.8 million, respectively, in CHIP redistribution funds. (Communication with the Centers for Medicare & Medicaid Services in May 2014.)

[79] The following 11 states meet the definition: Connecticut, Hawaii, Maryland, Minnesota, New Hampshire, New Mexico, Rhode Island, Tennessee, Vermont, Washington, and Wisconsin.

[80] §2015(g)(4) of the Social Security Act.

[81] The E-FMAP rate is not available for children aged 6 to 18 who have access to private health insurance.

[82] Centers for Medicare & Medicaid Services, Medicaid and CHIP FAQs: Funding for New Adult Group, Coverage of Former Foster Care Children and CHIP Financing, December 2013.

[83] See Tricia Brooks, Martha Heberlein, and Joseph Fu, Georgetown University Health Policy Institute, Center for Children and Families, Dismantling CHIP in Arizona: How Losing KidsCare Impacts a Child's Health Care Costs, May 2014; Anita Cardwell, et al., National Academy for State Health Policy and Georgetown University Health Policy Institute, Center for Children and Families; Benefits and Cost Sharing in Separate CHIP Programs, May 2014; and MACPAC, Report to Congress on Medicaid and CHIP, March 2015.

[84] Under CHIP and Medicaid, out-of-pocket spending (including both premiums and cost sharing) is exempt for many children and pregnant women, and when premiums and cost sharing apply, they cannot exceed 5% of the family's income. For the health insurance exchanges, in 2014, the out-of-pocket spending cannot exceed $6,350 for self-only coverage and $12,700 for coverage other than self-only.

[85] MACPAC, Report to Congress on Medicaid and CHIP, June 2014; Tricia Brooks, MACPAC Considers Future of CHIP, Georgetown University Health Policy Institute's Center for Children and Families, Say Ahhh! Blog, November 22, 2013.

[86] The policy options discussed herein reflect current law. They do not take into consideration the potential implications on the ACA coverage provisions from the forthcoming U.S. Supreme Court ruling in King v. Burwell or new legislation. For more information on the potential implications of the Court's decision in King v. Burwell, see CRS Report CRS Report R43833, Premium Tax Credits and Federal Health Insurance Exchanges: Questions and Answers, by Jennifer A. Staman et al.

[87] For more information about the ACA MOE requirement and CHIP, see CRS Report R43909, CHIP and the ACA Maintenance of Effort (MOE) Requirement: In Brief, by Alison Mitchell and Evelyne P. Baumrucker.

[88] §2105(d)(3) of the Social Security Act.

[89] The HHS Secretary has not issued guidance regarding the impact of the MOE requirements if federal CHIP funding were to expire.

[90] Both the CHIP MOE under §2105(d)(3) of the Social Security Act and the Medicaid MOE under §1902(gg)(2) of the Social Security Act concurrently apply to the CHIP Medicaid expansion programs.

[91] This option is only available to states if the HHS Secretary certifies that the coverage in the health insurance exchanges is "at least comparable" to CHIP in terms of benefits and cost sharing. However, some children will not be eligible for subsidized exchange coverage due to the "family glitch."

[92] Preliminary FY2014 CHIP enrollment data show about half of CHIP enrollees are in CHIP Medicaid expansion programs and about half are in separate CHIP programs. (MACPAC, Report to Congress on Medicaid and CHIP, March 2015.)

[93] CHIP children covered under CHIP Medicaid expansion programs are an optional eligibility group under Medicaid. However, because the Medicaid MOE for children extends through FY2019, states are not permitted to roll back Medicaid eligibility for these children without the loss of all Medicaid federal matching funds.

[94] See footnote 92.

[95] Subsidized coverage in the health insurance exchanges is not available to individuals with access to affordable health insurance. The "family glitch" results from the definition of affordable coverage. Under the ACA, employer-sponsored insurance is considered affordable if employees' premiums contributions for self-only coverage (not family coverage) comprise less than 9.5% of family income. However, there is no limit on the employees' share of premiums for family coverage. Due to the "family glitch," some of the current CHIP enrollees would not be eligible for subsidized coverage in the health insurance exchanges based on their parent's access to affordable employer-sponsored insurance. For more information about subsidized coverage in the health insurance exchanges, see CRS Report R41137, Health Insurance Premium Credits in the Patient Protection and Affordable Care Act (ACA) in 2014, by Bernadette Fernandez.

[96] For more information on this analysis, see MACPAC, Report to Congress on Medicaid and CHIP, March 2015.

[97] MACPAC, Report to Congress on Medicaid and CHIP, March 2015.

[98] Ibid.

[99] Ibid.

[100] Ibid.

[101] Premium tax credits are provided to certain individuals with household income between 100% and 400% FPL who do not have access to minimum essential coverage, and these individuals with income between 100% and 250% FPL could be eligible for cost-sharing subsidies.

[102] The definition of minimum essential coverage is broad. It includes Medicare Part A, Medicaid, the State Children's Health Insurance Program (CHIP), Tricare, the TRICARE for Life program, the veteran's health care program, the Peace Corps program, a government plan (local, state, federal) including the Federal Employees Health Benefits Program (FEHBP) and any plan established by an Indian tribal government, any plan offered in the individual, small group, or large group markets, a grandfathered health plan, and any other health benefits coverage, such as a state health benefits risk pool, as recognized by the HHS Secretary in coordination with the Treasury Secretary.

In: State Children's Health Insurance Program ISBN: 978-1-63483-675-3
Editor: Marty Sparks

Chapter 2

H.R. 2: THE MEDICARE ACCESS AND CHIP REAUTHORIZATION ACT OF 2015[*]

Jim Hahn and Kirstin B. Blom

SUMMARY

On March 26, 2015, the House passed H.R. 2, the Medicare Access and CHIP Reauthorization Act (MACRA) of 2015. This act would repeal the current sustainable growth rate (SGR) formula for calculating updates to Medicare payment rates to physicians and establish an alternative set of annual updates. In addition, MACRA would introduce a new merit-based incentive payment system and put in place processes for developing, evaluating, and adopting alternative payment models (APMs).

H.R. 2 also would extend funding for the Children's Health Insurance Program (CHIP) for two additional years. Currently, CHIP is funded through FY2015.

In addition to repealing the SGR (Title I) and extending funding for CHIP (Title III), the act also would make other health-related changes. Title II would extend several expiring provisions in the Medicare and Medicaid programs, including the qualifying individual (QI) program and the transitional medical assistance (TMA) program. Title IV includes Medicare program changes to offset the cost of repealing the SGR mechanism. These proposed offsets include limiting certain Medigap

---

[*] This is an edited, reformatted and augmented version of a Congressional Research Service publication, No. R43962, dated April 10, 2015.

policies and making adjustments to income-related premiums in Medicare Parts B and D and to inpatient hospital payment rates. Title V includes provisions related to program integrity in Medicare, including a prohibition on including Social Security numbers on beneficiaries' Medicare cards.

This report provides a brief summary of each provision of H.R. 2. Each summary includes a brief description of current law and an explanation of how the act would change current law.

OVERVIEW

On March 26, 2015, the House passed H.R. 2, the Medicare Access and CHIP Reauthorization Act (MACRA) of 2015. This act would repeal the current sustainable growth rate (SGR) formula for calculating updates to Medicare payment rates to physicians and establish an alternative set of annual updates. In addition, MACRA would introduce a new merit-based incentive payment system and put in place processes for developing, evaluating, and adopting alternative payment models (APMs).

H.R. 2 also would extend funding for the Children's Health Insurance Program (CHIP) for two additional years. Currently, CHIP is funded through FY2015.

In addition to repealing the SGR (Title I) and extending funding for CHIP (Title III), the act also would make other health-related changes. Title II would extend several expiring provisions in the Medicare and Medicaid programs, including the qualifying individual (QI) program and the transitional medical assistance (TMA) program. Title IV includes Medicare program changes to offset the cost of repealing the SGR mechanism. These proposed offsets include limiting certain Medigap policies and making adjustments to income-related premiums in Medicare Parts B and D and to inpatient hospital payment rates. Title V includes provisions related to program integrity in Medicare, including a prohibition on including Social Security numbers on beneficiaries' Medicare cards.

This report provides a brief summary of each provision of H.R. 2. Each summary includes a description of current law and an explanation of how the act would change current law. Please see the **Appendix** for a list of the abbreviations used throughout this report. The Congressional Budget Office (CBO) and the Joint Committee on Taxation (JCT) estimated the budgetary effects of H.R. 2.[1]

SUMMARY OF PROVISIONS

Title I—SGR Repeal and Medicare Provider Payment Modernization

Section 101: Repealing the Sustainable Growth Rate and Improving Medicare Payment for Physicians' Services

Background

Currently, Medicare payments for services of physicians and certain nonphysician practitioners are made on the basis of a fee schedule. The Medicare physician fee schedule (MPFS) assigns relative values to each of the approximately 7,500 service codes that reflect physician work (i.e., the time, skill, and intensity it takes to provide the service), practice expenses, and malpractice costs. The relative value for a service compares the relative work involved in performing one service with the work involved in providing other physicians' services. The scale used to compare the value of one service with another is known as a *resource-based relative value scale* (RBRVS). The relative values are adjusted for geographic variation in input costs. The adjusted relative values are then converted into a dollar payment amount by a conversion factor.

The Centers for Medicare & Medicaid Services (CMS), which is responsible for maintaining and updating the fee schedule, continually modifies and refines the methodology for estimating relative value units (RVUs). The American Medical Association/Specialty Society Relative Value Scale Update Committee (RUC) historically has provided advice and recommendations to CMS to assist in these assessments. CMS is required to review the RVUs no less than every five years.

In determining adjustments to RVUs used as the basis for calculating Medicare physician reimbursement under the fee schedule, the Secretary of Health and Human Services (HHS) has authority to adjust the number of RVUs for any service code to take into account changes in medical practice, coding changes, new data on relative value components, or the addition of new procedures. The Secretary of HHS is required to publish an explanation of the basis for such adjustments. These adjustments are subject to a budget neutrality condition. With the exception of certain expenditures that are exempt by statute, the adjustments may not cause the amount of expenditures made under the MPFS to differ from year to year by more than $20 million from the expenditures that would have been incurred without such an adjustment.

The Balanced Budget Act of 1997 (BBA97; P.L. 105-33) requires that, in developing the resource-based practice expense RVUs, the Secretary (1) use generally accepted cost accounting principles, to the maximum extent possible, that recognize all staff, equipment, supplies, and expenses, not solely those that can be linked to specific procedures and actual data on equipment utilization; (2) develop a refinement method to be used during the transition; and (3) consider, in the course of notice and comment rulemaking, impact projections that compare new proposed payment amounts to data on actual physician practice expense.

Created by BBA97, the sustainable growth rate (SGR) formula is the statutory method for determining the annual updates to the MPFS. The SGR methodology was established because of the concern that the Medicare fee schedule itself would not adequately constrain overall increases in spending for physicians' services. Generally, under the SGR formula, if cumulative expenditures from the current period going back to 1996 (the base year) are less than the cumulative spending target over the same period, the annual update is increased according to a statutory formula. However, if spending exceeds the cumulative spending target over the same period, the SGR methodology necessitates fee schedule update reductions to bring spending back in line with the target growth rate.

In the first few years of the SGR system, the actual expenditures did not exceed the targets and the updates to the physician fee schedule were close to the Medicare economic index (MEI, a price index of inputs required to produce physician services). Beginning in 2002, the cumulative actual expenditures exceeded allowed targets, resulting in SGR-mandated reductions in the update adjustment factor, and the discrepancy has grown with each year. However, with the exception of 2002, when a 4.8% decrease was applied, Congress has enacted a series of laws to override the reductions.

Most recently, the Protecting Access to Medicare Act (PAMA; P.L. 113-93) included a provision that averted the reduction and maintained the MPFS payments at current rates through March 31, 2015. CMS actuaries estimate that, without additional congressional intervention, the statutory change in the update factor would result in a 21% reduction in payment rates under the MPFS, keeping April 1, 2015.

The MPFS currently has several modifications and adjustments that depend on actions taken by the physician with regard to reporting quality data. The Tax Relief and Health Care Act of 2006 (TRHCA; P.L. 109-432) required the establishment of a physician quality reporting system that would include an incentive payment to eligible professionals who satisfactorily report data on quality measures, based on a percentage of the allowed Medicare charges for covered professional services. The Medicare Improvements for Patients and Providers Act of 2008 (MIPPA; P.L. 110-275) made this program permanent and extended the bonuses through 2010; the incentive payment was increased from 1.5% of total allowable charges under the physician fee schedule in 2007 and 2008 to 2% in 2009 and 2010. The Patient Protection and Affordable Care Act (ACA; P.L. 111-148, as amended) extended quality measure reporting incentive payments through 2014 and put in place a penalty for providers who do not report quality measures beginning in 2015. Similarly, the bonus payment for meaningful use of electronic health records eventually becomes a penalty for those who do not meet the criteria.

As a result of changes in MIPPA and the ACA, eligible professionals who successfully reported in 2010 received a 1% bonus in 2011; those who successfully reported in 2011, 2012, and 2013 received a 0.5% bonus in 2012, 2013, and 2014, respectively. In contrast, eligible professionals who fail to participate successfully in the program face a 1.5% payment penalty in 2015 and a 2% payment penalty in 2016 and in subsequent years. The incentive payments and adjustments in payment will be based on the allowed charges for all covered services furnished by the eligible professional, based on the applicable percentage of the fee schedule amount.

Both the Medicare Payment Advisory Commission (MedPAC) and the Government Accountability Office (GAO) have suggested that CMS provide information to physicians on their resource use with the expectation that physicians who are outliers would alter their practice patterns in response. MedPAC asserts that physicians would be able to assess their practice styles, evaluate whether they tend to use more resources than their peers or what evidence-based research (if available) recommends, and revise practice styles as appropriate. MIPPA (§131(c)) established such a physician feedback program. The program uses Medicare claims data and other data to provide confidential feedback reports to physicians (and as determined appropriate by the Secretary, to groups of physicians) that measure the resources involved in furnishing care to Medicare beneficiaries. CMS initially called this effort the Physician Resource Use Feedback Program but has renamed this initiative the Physician Resource Use Measurement and Reporting Program.

Incentives for the adoption and "meaningful use" of electronic health records (EHR) also modify payments under the MPFS. The American Recovery and Reinvestment Act (ARRA; P.L. 111-5) authorized incentive payments over a five-year period through Medicare Part B to physicians who are meaningful users of certified EHR technology. *Meaningful use* is defined as (1) demonstrating to the satisfaction of the Secretary the use of certified EHR technology in a meaningful manner (including e-prescribing), including for the purpose of exchanging electronic health information to improve health care quality; and (2) using such certified EHR technology to report clinical quality measures, as selected by the Secretary. The incentive payments equal 75% of the allowed Part B charges during the reporting year. However, the total amount that a physician could receive is capped and decreases over time. For EHR adopters in 2011 and 2012, eligible physicians received up to $18,000 in the first payment year, $12,000 in the second year, $8,000 in the third year, $4,000 in the fourth year, and $2,000 in the fifth, and final, year. For eligible physicians practicing in health professional shortage areas, the incentive payment amounts are increased by 10%.

Eligible physicians first becoming meaningful EHR users after 2012 received fewer payments, and those who did not adopt EHRs until after 2014 received no bonus. No incentive payments will be made after 2016. Incentive payments are not available for hospital-based physicians. Eligible physicians who are not meaningful users of certified HIT systems by 2015 will see their Medicare payments reduced by the following amounts: 1% in 2015, 2% in 2016, and 3% in 2017 and in each subsequent year. For 2018 and each subsequent year, if the proportion of eligible physicians who are meaningful EHR users is less than 75%, the payment reduction will be further decreased by one percentage point from the applicable amount in the previous year, though the reduction cannot exceed 5%. The Secretary may, on a case-by-case basis, exempt eligible physicians (e.g., rural physicians that lack sufficient Internet access) from the payment reduction for up to five years if it is determined that being a meaningful EHR user would result in significant hardship.

MPFS payments, based on fee for service, have been criticized for rewarding volume of care without incentivizing quality or improved outcomes. Although payments vary across geography by design and sometimes are modified to satisfy a policy objective, such as when providing an incentive for physicians to provide care in underserved areas or to meet quality reporting metrics, historically payments have not varied with respect to quality or efficiency.

The ACA required the Secretary to establish and apply a separate, budget-neutral payment modifier to the MPFS. The separate value-based payment modifier is to be based on the relative quality and cost of the care provided by physicians or physician groups. Quality of care is to be evaluated on a composite of risk-adjusted measures of quality established by the Secretary, such as measures that reflect health outcomes. Costs, defined as expenditures per individual, are to be evaluated based on a composite of appropriate measures of costs established by the Secretary that eliminate the effect of geographic adjustments in payment rates and take into account risk factors (such as socioeconomic and demographic characteristics, ethnicity, and health status of individuals) and other factors determined appropriate by the Secretary.

Beginning January 1, 2015, the value-based payment modifier applies for items and services furnished for physicians in groups of 100 or more eligible professionals who submit claims to Medicare under a single tax identification number. By 2017, the value-based payment modifier will apply to all physicians who participate in fee-for-service (FFS) Medicare. The Secretary is to apply the payment modifier in a manner that promotes systems-based care and takes into account the special circumstances of physicians or groups of physicians in rural areas and other underserved communities.

Overview

This provision of H.R. 2 would make fundamental changes to the way Medicare payments to physicians are determined, how they are updated, and how they incentivize physicians. The bill would (1) repeal the SGR methodology for determining updates to the MPFS and establish annual fee updates in the short term and put in place a new method for determining updates afterward; (2) establish a merit-based incentive payment system (MIPS) to consolidate and replace several existing incentive programs; (3) incentivize the development of, and participation, in alternative payment models (APMs); and (4) make other changes to Medicare physician payment statutes.

Payment Updates

For the first few years after enactment, the bill would set the annual MPFS payment updates. From January 2015 through June 2015, the update would be 0%; for the remainder of the year— July 2015 through December 2015, the payments would be increased by 0.5%. In each of the next four years, 2016 through 2019, the payment increase would be 0.5% each year. For the next six years, from 2020 through 2025, the payment update would be 0%.

Beginning in 2026, there would be two update factors, one for items and services furnished by a participant in a new APM (see below) and another for those who do not participate in an APM. The update factor for the APM participants would be 0.75%, and the update factor for those not participating in an APM would be 0.25%.

MedPAC would prepare reports to assist Congress in evaluating the changes. By July 1, 2017, MedPAC would be required to submit a report to Congress on the relationship between (1) utilization of physician and other health professional services and Medicare expenditures on items and services, and (2) total utilization and expenditures and their rates of increase under Medicare Parts A, B, and D. The report would include a methodology to describe the relationship between the practice and ordering patterns of physician and other health professionals and total utilization and expenditure of healthcare services in Medicare Part A, B, and D. A final report would be due to Congress by July 1, 2021. A second report, due no later than July 1, 2019, would examine the effect of the 2015 though 2019 payment updates on the efficiency, economy, and quality of care provided, determine whether the update ensured a sufficient number of providers to maintain access to care by Medicare beneficiaries, and make recommendations for future payment updates to ensure adequate access.

Merit-Based Incentive Payment System

The provision would create a new incentive payment system while sunsetting several existing programs on the last day of 2018: (1) the meaningful use incentive program for certified electronic health record (EHR) technology, (2) the quality reporting incentive program currently called PQRI, and (3) the value-based payment modifier. The Secretary would establish a replacement program, the merit-based incentive payment system (MIPS) that would accomplish the following:

- develop a methodology for assessing the total performance of each MIPS-eligible professional according to performance standards described below;
- use the methodology above to provide for a composite performance score as specified below for each professional for each performance period; and
- use the composite performance score of the MIPS-eligible professional to make MIPS program incentive payments (as described below) to the professional for the year.

The MIPS program would apply to payments for items and services furnished on or after January 1, 2019.

The types of health care professionals eligible for the MIPS incentive payments would change over time. Subject to the exclusions and definitions of newly eligible participants described below, only physicians, as defined under current law as well as physician assistants, nurse practitioners, clinical nurse specialists, and certified registered nurse anesthetists—including groups that included such professionals—would be eligible for MIPS program incentives in the first and second years for which the MIPS program would apply. The Secretary would decide which other health care professionals, in addition to those already specified, would be eligible in subsequent years. Health care professionals excluded from the MIPS incentive payment program would include otherwise eligible professionals who (1) would be qualifying APM participants (as defined below), (2) would be partial qualifying APM participants (as defined below), and (3) would not exceed the low-volume threshold measurement.

With the sunsetting of the incentive programs mentioned above, the MIPS program would use a new set of measures and activities under four performance categories to determine whether an individual qualified for an incentive payment. A composite performance score would be calculated for each MIPS-eligible professional, which would be used to determine the incentive payment. The Secretary would use the following performance categories to determine the composite performance score.

- *Quality*. The final quality measures under current law for existing incentive payments for quality reporting and quality of care.
- *Resource use*. The measures of resource use established for the value-based modifier under current law and, to the extent feasible, accounting for the cost of Part D drugs.
- *Clinical practice improvement activities*. The clinical practice improvement activities would be specified by the Secretary and would include at least the following subcategories:
    a) expanded practice access, such as same-day appointments for urgent needs and after-hours access to clinician advice;
    b) population management, such as monitoring health conditions of individuals to provide timely health care or participation in a qualified clinical data registry;

c) care coordination, such as timely communication of test results, timely exchange of clinical information to patients and other providers, and use of remote monitoring or telehealth;
d) beneficiary engagement, such as the establishment of care plans for individuals with complex care needs and beneficiary self-management assessment and training, and using shared decisionmaking mechanisms;
e) patient safety and practice assessment, such as thorough use of clinical or surgical checklists and practice assessments related to maintaining certification; and
f) participation in an alternative payment model.

In establishing the clinical practice improvement activities, the Secretary would give consideration to the circumstances of small practices (15 or fewer professionals) and practices located in rural areas and in health professional shortage areas.

- *Meaningful use of certified EHR technology*. The requirements established under current law for determining whether an eligible professional is a meaningful EHR user.

By November 1 of each year, the Secretary would establish and publish in the *Federal Register* an annual list of quality measures from which MIPS-eligible professionals could choose, to serve as the basis for the MIPS payment adjustment. The list would be updated to remove measures that are no longer meaningful (e.g., when a measure is topped out) and to add new quality measures.

The Secretary would establish MIPS performance standards and the performance period with respect to the measures and activities. The performance standards would take into account historical performance standards, improvement, and the opportunity for continued improvement. The Secretary would establish a performance period for each year in which incentive payments would be determined, beginning with 2019; the performance period would begin and end prior to the beginning of the year in which the incentive payments would be paid.

The Secretary would develop a methodology for assessing the total performance of each MIPSeligible professional according to the performance standards and the applicable measures and activities specified above and determine a composite assessment (*composite performance score*) for each such professional for each performance period. As incentive, the Secretary would treat those eligible professionals who fail to report on an applicable measure or activity that is required as achieving the lowest potential score applicable.

In weighting the performance categories to determine the composite performance score, 30% of the initial score would be based on performance on the quality measure; outcome measures would be encouraged, as feasible. The weight for the resource use category also would be 30% initially, and the clinical practice category would receive a weight of 15%. The meaningful use of certified EHR technology would receive a 25% weight. These weights would change over time. For example, should the percentage of meaningful EHR users exceed 75%, the Secretary could reduce the weight for that category, but not below 15%, with the other weights increased appropriately.

The Secretary would be given flexibility in weighting performance categories, measures, and activities. The Secretary may assign different scoring weights (including a weight of zero) for (1) each performance category based on the extent to which the category is applicable to the type of eligible professional involved, and (2) each measure or activity based on the extent to which the measure or activity is applicable to the type of eligible professional involved.

The Secretary would specify an MIPS program incentive payment adjustment factor for each MIPS-eligible professional for a year, which would be determined by the composite performance score of the eligible professional for the year. The application of the adjustment factors would result in differential payments reflecting the professional's composite performance score relative to an established performance threshold. Professionals with composite scores at the threshold would receive no adjustment; higher composite scores would receive higher adjustments and composite performance scores below the threshold would lead to a negative adjustment. The MIPS adjustment factor (positive or negative) would be 4% in 2019, 5% in 2020, 7% in 2021, and 9% in 2022 and in subsequent years; each professional's MIPS adjustment factor would be between 0% and +/– (adjustment factor)%, reflecting his or her composite score between 0 and 100 on a sliding scale.

An additional MIPS adjustment could be earned for exceptional performance. For years 2019 through 2024, eligible professionals with a composite performance score at or above the additional performance threshold could receive an additional positive MIPS adjustment factor that would vary with the amount by which the score exceeds the threshold, to be specified by the Secretary.

The performance threshold would be the mean or median (as selected by the Secretary) of the composite performance scores for all MIPS-eligible professionals; the Secretary could reassess the selection of the mean or the median every three years. The exceptional performance threshold would be determined in one of two ways: (1) the score equal to the 25th percentile of the range of possible composite scores higher than the performance threshold above, or (2) the score equal to the 25th percentile of the actual composite scores for MIPS-eligible professionals with scores at or higher than the performance threshold above. For the first two years to which the MIPS applies, the Secretary would establish the two thresholds based on (1) information from a period prior to the performance period, (2) data available with respect to performance on measures and activities that may be used in the four MIPS performance categories, and (3) other factors the Secretary determines to be appropriate. Beginning with 2019, the payment received by a MIPS-eligible professional would be the amount otherwise paid (under the MPFS) multiplied by the MIPS adjustment factor expressed as a percentage.

The estimated aggregate increase in payments for additional MIPS adjustments for exceptional performance is to be $500 million for each year from 2019 through 2024, subject to the restriction that the additional adjustment cannot exceed 10% for an eligible professional in a year. Thus, the aggregate increase in payments may be less than $500 million if this restriction is applied. Each MIPS-eligible professional would be notified as to his or her MIPS adjustment factor (including the additional adjustment factor for exceptional performance) no later than December 2 (30 days prior to January 1) of the year before the adjustment factor would be applied. The MIPS adjustment factor(s) would apply only with respect to the year involved, and the Secretary would not take such adjustments into account in making payments to a MIPS-eligible professional in a subsequent year.

The Secretary would make information regarding the performance of MIPS-eligible professionals under the MIPS program available to the public, in an easily understandable format on CMS's Physician Compare Internet website. This information would include the composite score for each MIPS-eligible professional and the performance of each MIPS-eligible professional with respect to each performance category, and could include each eligible professional's performance on each measure or activity in the four performance categories. This information would indicate, where appropriate, that publicized information may not be representative of the eligible professional's entire patient population, the variety of services furnished by the eligible professional, or the health conditions of individuals treated. The

Secretary would provide for an opportunity for an eligible professional to review and submit corrections for his or her information prior to such information being made public. The Secretary would periodically post aggregate information on the MIPS program on the Physician Compare Internet website, including the range of composite scores for all MIPS-eligible professionals and the range of the performance of all MIPS-eligible professionals with respect to each performance category.

The Secretary would consult with stakeholders in carrying out the MIPS program, including for the identification of performance category measures and activities and the methodologies for developing the composite score and regarding the use of qualified clinical data registries. These consultations would include the use of requests for information or other mechanisms determined appropriate.

To provide technical assistance to small practices and practices in health professional shortage areas, the Secretary would enter into contracts or agreements with appropriate entities (such as quality improvement organizations, regional extension centers, or regional health collaboratives) to offer guidance and assistance to MIPS-eligible professionals in practices of 15 or fewer professionals with priority given to professionals located in rural areas, health professional shortage areas, or practices with low composite scores. The guidance and assistance would be provided with respect to the performance categories or with respect to how to transition to the implementation of and participation in an alternative payment model (as specified below).

For purposes of implementing the technical assistance program, $20 million from the Federal Supplementary Medical Insurance (SMI) Trust Fund would be made available to CMS for each of FY2016-FY2020. These amounts would be available until expended.

To provide feedback to eligible professionals to improve performance, beginning July 1, 2017, the Secretary would make available timely (such as quarterly) confidential feedback to each MIPS-eligible professional on the individual's performance with respect to the quality and resource-use performance categories. Information on the clinical practice improvement activities and meaningful EHR use categories could also be provided. The Secretary could use one or more mechanisms to provide this feedback, including a web-based portal or other mechanisms determined appropriate by the Secretary.

The Secretary could use data from periods prior to the current performance period with respect to MIPS-eligible professionals and could use rolling periods to make illustrative calculations about the performance of these professionals. This feedback would be exempt from disclosure under the Freedom of Information Act.

Beginning July 1, 2018, the Secretary would make available to each MIPS-eligible professional information about items and services furnished to the professional's patients by other suppliers and providers of services. This information would include the following: (1) the name of each provider furnishing items and services to such patients during the period, the types of items and services so furnished, and the dates these items and services were furnished, and (2) historical data, such as averages and other measures of the distribution if appropriate, of the total allowed charges as well as the components of the charges, as well as other figures as determined appropriate by the Secretary.

The Secretary would establish a process under which an MIPS-eligible professional could seek an informal review of the calculation of the individual's MIPS program incentive payment. The results of such a review would not be taken into account for purposes of determining the MIPS adjustment factor and payments with respect to a year (other than with respect to the calculation of the eligible professional's MIPS program incentive payment for such year).

There would be no administrative or judicial review of the following:

- the methodology used to determine the amount of the MIPS adjustment factors, including for exceptional performance,
- the establishment of the performance standards and the performance period,
- the identification of performance category measures and activities and information made public or posted on the Physician Compare Internet website of CMS, or
- the methodology developed and used to calculate performance scores and the calculation of such scores, including the weighting of measures and activities under such methodology.

The Comptroller General of the United States (GAO) would submit four MIPS program evaluation reports to Congress. The first report, due October 1, 2021, would (1) examine the distribution of the composite performance scores and MIPS adjustment factors and their patterns, including an analysis of the scores and factors across types of provider, practice size, geographic location, and patient mix, (2) provide recommendations for improving the MIPS program, (3) evaluate the impact of technical assistance funding on the ability of professionals to improve within the MIPS program or to transition successfully to an alternative payment model, with priority for evaluation given to practices located in rural areas, health professional shortage areas, and medically underserved areas, and (4) provide recommendations for optimizing the use of such technical assistance funds.

The second GAO report, due 18 months after enactment, would examine the alignment of quality measures used in public and private programs by (1) comparing the similarities and differences in the use of quality measures under the original Medicare FFS program under Parts A and B, the Medicare Advantage program, and private payer arrangements, and (2) making recommendations on how to reduce administrative burden involved in applying such quality measures.

The third GAO report, due January 1, 2017, would study the role of independent risk managers and examine whether entities that pool financial risk for physician practices, such as independent risk managers, can play a role in supporting physician practices, particularly small physician practices, in assuming financial risk for the treatment of patients. The report would examine barriers that small physician practices currently face in assuming financial risk for treating patients, the types of risk management entities that could assist physician practices in participating in two-sided risk payment models, and how such entities could assist with risk management and with quality improvement activities. The report also would include an analysis of any existing legal barriers to such arrangements.

The fourth GAO report, due October 1, 2021, would examine the transition of professionals in rural areas, health professional shortage areas, or medically underserved areas to an alternative payment model. The report would make recommendations for removing administrative barriers to practices to participate in such models, including small practices consisting of 15 or fewer professionals, in rural areas, health professional shortage areas, and medically underserved areas.

To implement the MIPS program and the related activities described above, $80 million would be transferred to CMS from the SMI Trust Fund for each fiscal year from 2015 through 2019; these funds would be available until expended.

The bill would make modifications to improve quality reporting for constructing MIPS composite scores. The existing physician feedback program would be succeeded by reports under the MIPS program beginning in

2018, and the meaningful EHR use clinical quality measure reporting requirement would be combined with the MIPS program.

Alternative Payment Models

In addition to creating the MIPS, which modifies but is still fundamentally based on FFS payment, this bill also would establish pathways for implementing new payment models that might eventually replace traditional FFS-based payment.

The term *alternative payment model* (APM) would be defined to mean any of the following:

- A model under the Center for Medicaid and Medicare Innovation (other than a health care innovation award);
- A Medicare shared savings program accountable care organization;
- A demonstration under Section 1866C of the Social Security Act (SSA);
- A demonstration required by federal law.

The term *eligible alternative payment entity* would mean an entity that (1) participates in an APM that requires participants to use certified EHR technology and provides for payment for covered professional services based on quality measures comparable to measures under the performance category described in the MIPS program established above, and (2) bears financial risk for monetary losses under the APM that are in excess of a nominal amount, or is a medical home expanded under Section 1115(c) of the SSA.

A *qualifying APM participant* would mean the following:

- For 2019 and 2020, an eligible professional for whom the Secretary determines that at least 25% of payments for Medicare-covered professional services furnished by a professional during the most recent period for which data are available (which could be less than a year) were attributable to services furnished to Medicare beneficiaries through an entity eligible for participation in an eligible alternative payment model (APM),
- For 2021 and 2022, an eligible professional who meets either of the following criteria:
    a) *Medicare payment threshold.* At least 50% of Medicare payments for covered professional services during the most recent period

for which data are available were furnished to Medicare beneficiaries through an eligible APM; or

b) *Combination all-payer and Medicare payment threshold.* Satisfies conditions on (1) the amount of Medicare payments made under qualified APMs and (2) payments made by other payers under arrangements in which quality measures, EHR technology, and other conditions apply.

- For 2023 and in subsequent years, an eligible professional as described above, but meeting a criteria of 75% for (a) and a similarly higher condition for (b).

A *partial qualifying APM participant* would be defined as an eligible professional who would fail to meet the appropriate revenue threshold to achieve a bonus payment under the qualified APM program but had achieved a lower threshold. The Secretary would select one of the following low-volume threshold measurements to determine the above exclusion for the performance period:

- a minimum number of Medicare beneficiaries who are treated by the eligible professional;
- a minimum number of items and services furnished by the professional; or
- a minimum amount of allowed charges billed by the professional.

In each case, the minimum number would be determined by the Secretary.

To advise and evaluate the development of alternative payment models, the bill would establish an ad hoc committee to be known as the Physician-Focused Payment Models Technical Advisory Committee. The committee would provide comments and recommendations to the Secretary as to whether the alternative payment models meet the criteria (to be established by the Secretary) for assessing physician-focused payment models.

The committee would be composed of 11 members appointed by the Comptroller General, and it would include individuals with national recognition for their expertise in physician-focused payment models and related delivery of care. No more than five members of the committee would be providers of services or suppliers or their representatives. Federal employees would not be allowed to be members of the committee. Members of the committee would be required to publicly disclose financial and other potential conflicts of interest. The initial appointments, to be made no later than 180 days after enactment, would be staggered, with three years being the length of a full term. Vacancies would be filled in the same manner as original appointments. Committee members would serve without compensation (travel expenses would be allowed), and the committee would meet as needed.

The HHS Assistant Secretary for Planning and Evaluation would provide technical and operational support for the committee, which could be by use of a contractor. The Office of the Actuary of the Centers for Medicare & Medicaid Services would provide actuarial assistance as needed. To establish and operate the committee, the Secretary would transfer amounts as necessary from the SMI Trust Fund, not to exceed $5 million for each fiscal year beginning in 2015.

The creation and recognition of alternative payment models under the Medicare program would follow a process of submission, review, and evaluation. By November 1, 2016, the Secretary would establish through rulemaking the criteria for physician-focused payment models, including models for specialist physicians that the committee could use for making comments and recommendations. During the comment period for the proposed rule, MedPAC could submit comments to the Secretary on the proposed criteria. The Secretary could update the criteria through rulemaking. Individuals and stakeholder entities also could submit proposals to the committee for physician-focused payment models that they believe meet the criteria. The committee would review models submitted on a periodic basis and provide comments and recommendations to the Secretary regarding whether the models meet the criteria. The Secretary would review the committee's comments and recommendations and post a detailed response on the CMS website.

Eligible Medicare professionals would be incentivized to participate in Medicare APMs through higher payments. Beginning in 2019 and ending in 2024, eligible professionals in a qualifying APM (see below) providing covered services would receive payment for the services provided that year as well as an amount equal to 5% of the estimated aggregate payment amounts for covered professional services for the preceding year. The incentive payment would be made in a lump sum on an annual basis, as soon as practicable. These incentive payments would not be taken into account for purposes of determining actual expenditures under an alternative payment model or for purposes of determining or rebasing any benchmarks used under the APM.

There would be no administrative or judicial review of the following:

- The determination that an eligible professional is a qualifying APM participant as described above and the determination that an entity is an eligible alternative payment entity.
- The determination of the amount of the 5% payment incentive for participation in APMs.

To encourage the development and testing of certain APMs, demonstration project authority regarding the testing of models (§1115A(b)(2) of the SSA) is amended to allow for models focusing

- primarily on physicians' services, with particular focus on such services furnished by physicians who are not primary care practitioners,
- on practices of 15 or fewer professionals,
- on risk-based models for small physician practices that may involve two-sided risk and prospective patient assignment, and that examine risk-adjusted decreases in mortality rates, hospital readmissions rates, and other relevant and appropriate clinical measures, and
- primarily on Medicaid, working in conjunction with the Center for Medicaid and CHIP Services.

The demonstration authority is also modified to add "statewide payment models" in addition to "other public sector or private sector payers" as factors for consideration.

The provision would require additional studies regarding the development and testing of APMs. By July 1, 2016, the Secretary would submit to Congress a study examining the feasibility of integrating APMs in the Medicare Advantage payment system; the study would include the feasibility of including a value-based modifier and whether such a modifier should be budget neutral. No later than two years after enactment, the Secretary, in consultation with the HHS inspector general (IG), would submit a study that would (1) examine the applicability of the federal fraud prevention laws to items and services furnished under the Medicare program for which payment is made under an APM; (2) identify aspects of APMs that are vulnerable to fraudulent activity; and (3) examine the implications of waivers to such laws granted in support of APMs, including under any potential expansion of APMs. The report would include recommendations for actions to be taken to reduce the vulnerability of such APMs to fraudulent activity and, as appropriate, recommendations of the IG for changes in federal fraud prevention laws to reduce such vulnerability.

Development of New Classification Codes

To improve the measurement of resource use—and to involve physician, practitioner, and other stakeholder communities in enhancing the infrastructure for resource use measurement— including for purposes of the MIPS and the APMs as added by this provision, the bill would require the development of (1) care episode and patient condition groups and classification codes, (2) patient relationship categories and codes to facilitate the attribution of patients and episodes to physicians or applicable practitioners, (3) expanded claims to gather more information for resource use measurement, and (4) a methodology for resource use analysis.

To classify similar patients into care episode groups and patient condition groups, the Secretary would be required to develop new classification codes. No later than 180 days after enactment, the Secretary would post a list of episode groups and related descriptive information as developed pursuant to the episode grouper (under current law). For 120 days after such posting, the Secretary would accept suggestions from physician specialty societies, applicable practitioner organizations, and other stakeholders for episode groups in addition to those posted as well as specific clinical criteria and patient characteristics in order to classify patients into care episode groups and patient condition groups. Taking into account this information, the Secretary would (1) establish care episode groups and patient condition groups that account for a target of an estimated one-half of Part A and Part B expenditures (with the target increasing over time as appropriate), and (2) assign codes to the groups.

In establishing the care episode groups, the Secretary would take into account the patient's clinical problems at the time items and services are furnished during an episode of care, such as the patient's clinical conditions or diagnoses, whether or not inpatient hospitalization occurs, and the principal procedures or services furnished, and other factors as appropriate.

In establishing the patient condition groups, the Secretary would take into account the patient's clinical history at the time of the medical visit, such as the patient's combination of chronic conditions, current health status, and recent significant history (such as hospitalization and major surgery during a previous period, such as three months), and other factors as appropriate, such as eligibility for Medicare and Medicaid.

The Secretary would draft a list of the care episode and patient condition codes (and the criteria and characteristics assigned to the codes) on the CMS website no later than 270 days after the end of the comment period. For 120 days after posting the list, the Secretary would seek comments from physician specialty societies, applicable practitioner organizations, and other stakeholders including representatives of Medicare beneficiaries, regarding the care episode and patient condition groups and codes. The Secretary would use mechanisms in addition to notice and comment rulemaking that could include the use of open door forums, town hall meetings, or other appropriate mechanisms. No later than 270 days after the end of the comment period, the Secretary would post an operational list of care episode and patient condition codes (and the criteria and characteristics assigned to the codes) on the CMS website.

The Secretary would revise the lists through rulemaking no later than November 1 of each year. The revisions could be based on experience, new information developed pursuant to the episode grouper, and input from the physician specialty societies, applicable practitioner organizations, and other stakeholders.

To develop patient relationship categories and codes to facilitate the attribution of patients and episodes to physicians or applicable practitioners, the Secretary would develop patient relationship categories and codes that define and distinguish the relationship and responsibility of a physician or applicable practitioner with a patient at the time an item or service is furnished. These patient relationship categories would include different relationships of the physician or practitioner to the patient (and the codes could reflect combinations of such categories). Examples of such relationship categories might include a physician or practitioner who

- considers himself or herself to have the primary responsibility for the general and ongoing care for the patient over extended periods of time;
- considers himself or herself to be the lead physician or practitioner and furnishes items and services and coordinates care furnished by other physicians or practitioners for the patient during an acute episode;
- furnishes items and services to the patient on a continuing basis during an acute episode of care, but in a supportive rather than a lead role;

- furnishes items and services to the patient on an occasional basis, usually at the request of another physician or practitioner; or
- furnishes items and services only as ordered by another physician or practitioner.

No later than one year after enactment, the Secretary would post a draft list of the patient relationship categories and codes on the CMS website. For 120 days after posting the list, the Secretary would seek comments from physician specialty societies, applicable practitioner organizations, and other stakeholders, including representatives of Medicare beneficiaries, regarding the patient relationship categories and codes. The Secretary would use mechanisms in addition to notice and comment rulemaking that could include the use of open-door forums, town-hall meetings, or other appropriate mechanisms. No later than 240 days after the end of the comment period, the Secretary would post an operational list of patient relationship categories and codes on the CMS website.

The Secretary would revise the lists through rulemaking no later than November 1 of each year. The revisions could be based on experience, new information developed pursuant to the episode grouper, and input from the physician specialty societies, applicable practitioner organizations, and other stakeholders.

To gather more information for resource use measurement, the Secretary would require that Medicare claims submitted on or after January 1, 2018, include the applicable codes as established above and the national provider identifier of the ordering physician or applicable practitioner (if different from the billing physician or applicable practitioner).

To evaluate the resources used to treat patients (with respect to care episode and patient condition groups) the Secretary would, as appropriate, (1) use the patient relationship codes reported on claims to attribute patients to one or more physicians and practitioners, (2) use the care episode and patient condition codes reported on claims as a basis to compare similar patients and care episodes and patient condition groups, and (3) conduct an analysis of resource use with respect to care episodes and patient condition groups of such patients. In conducting an analysis with respect to patients attributed to physicians and providers as specified above, the Secretary would (1) use the claims data experience of patients by the patient condition codes during a common period, such as 12 months, and (2) use the claims data experience of patients by care episode codes in the case of episodes both with and without hospitalization.

In measuring the resource use, the Secretary would use per patient total allowed charges for all Medicare Part A and Part B services (and Part D, if appropriate) for the analysis of patient resource use, by care episode codes and by patient condition codes. The Secretary could use other measures of allowed charges (such as subtotals for categories of items and services) and measures of utilization of items and services (such as frequency of specific items and services and the ratio of specific items and services among attributed patients or episodes). The Secretary would seek comments regarding the resource use methodology.

Section 102: Priorities and Funding for Measure Development

Section 931 of the Public Health Service Act (PHSA; P.L. 78-410) (42 U.S.C. 299b-31) and Section 1890A(e) (42 U.S.C. 1395aaa-1) of the SSA, as added by Section 2013 of the ACA, require (1) the Secretary of HHS to award grants and contracts to eligible entities for purposes of developing, improving, updating, or expanding quality measures, as specified; and (2) the Administrator of CMS to develop quality and efficiency measures for use under the SSA through the awarding of contracts. In addition, Section 931 of the PHSA requires the Secretary to develop provider-level outcome measures for hospitals and physicians and, specifically, 10 outcome measures each for acute and chronic diseases and primary and preventive care.

This provision of H.R. 2 would amend Section 1848 of the SSA to add a new subsection (s), "Priorities and Funding for Quality Measure Development." The Secretary would be required, not later than January 1, 2016, to develop a draft plan for the development of quality measures under applicable provisions, as specified. Such plan would be required to address how measures used in integrated delivery systems and by private payers could be incorporated under Title XVIII; how coordination of measure development would occur; and how clinical guidelines should be used in measure development. It would be required to consider gaps analyses, as specified; whether measures apply across health care settings; clinical practice improvement activities; and quality domains, as specified. In addition, the plan would be required to prioritize, among other things, outcome, patient experience, care coordination, and appropriate use measures. The Secretary would be required to accept stakeholder comments through March 1, 2016, on the draft plan and would be required to post on the CMS website not later than May 1, 2016, an operational plan for the development of quality measures for use as specified. This plan would be required to be updated as appropriate.

The Secretary also would be required to enter into contracts or other arrangements to develop, improve, update, or expand quality measures, in accordance with the plan. In entering into contracts, the Secretary would be required to give priority to developing measures of outcomes, patient experience of care, and care coordination, among other things, and would be required to consider whether measures developed would be electronically specified and relevant clinical practice guidelines, to the extent they exist.

The Secretary would be required, not later than May 1, 2017, and annually thereafter, to post on the CMS website a report on the progress made in developing quality measures for application as specified. The reports would be required to include the following: (1) a description of the Secretary's efforts to implement the subsection; (2) information about measures developed over the previous year, as specified; (3) information about measures currently in development, as specified; (4) a description of any updates to the plan, including newly identified gaps, as well as the inventory of measures applicable, as specified; and (5) other information as the Secretary determines would be appropriate.

The Secretary would be required to seek stakeholder input with respect to (1) the identification of gaps where no measures exist, and specifically with respect to measures of outcomes, patient experience of care, care coordination, and overuse; (2) prioritization of quality measure development to address such gaps; and (3) other quality measure development areas, as determined by the Secretary.

The Secretary would be required to provide for the transfer of $15 million, for each of fiscal years 2015 through 2019, from the Federal Supplementary Medical Insurance Trust Fund to the CMS Program Management Account. The funds would remain available through FY2022. The Paperwork Reduction Act of 1980 (44 U.S.C. 35) would not apply to information collection for measure development activities.

Section 103: Encouraging Care Management for Individuals with Chronic Care Needs

Prior CMS regulations have established payment for chronic care management (CCM) services under the Medicare Part B physician fee schedule. Under these regulations, beginning January 1, 2015, CMS would allow a physician or qualified health practitioner (QHP) to be reimbursed under the Medicare physician fee schedule (MPFS) for providing CCM services per calendar month to patients with two or more chronic conditions. Specifically, the chronic conditions are expected to last at least 12 months (or until the death of the patient) and place the patient at significant risk of death, acute exacerbation/decompensation, or functional decline. The patient also must be residing at his or her home or in a domiciliary, rest home, or assisted living facility.

This provision of H.R. 2 would codify in statute existing CMS initiatives with respect to CCM services and provide other requirements for such services. This provision would require the Secretary to make payment under the MPFS for CCM services provided by a physician, physician assistant, nurse practitioner, clinical nurse specialist, or certified nurse midwife furnished on or after January 1, 2015. Additionally, this provision would require that payment for CCM services (1) could not be made to more than one applicable provider for such services, (2) could not be duplicative of payment that is otherwise made by Medicare, and (3) would not require that an annual wellness visit or an initial preventive physical examination be furnished as a condition of payment.

This provision of H.R. 2 also would require the Secretary to conduct an education and outreach campaign to inform professionals who provide Part B services and beneficiaries enrolled in Part B of the benefits for CCM services and to encourage individuals with chronic care needs to receive such care. This campaign would be directed by the Office of Rural Health Policy within HHS and the Office of Minority Health within CMS, and it would focus on encouraging participation by underserved, rural populations and racial/ethnic minority populations. No later than December 31, 2017, the Secretary would be required to submit a report to Congress on the use of CCM services by individuals in underserved, rural populations and racial/ethnic minority populations. The report would identify barriers to receiving CCM services and make recommendations for increasing the appropriate use of CCM services.

Section 104: Empowering Beneficiary Choices Through Continued Access to Information on Physicians' Services

Section 10331 of the ACA required the Secretary of HHS to develop, not later than January 1, 2011, a Physician Compare website with information about physicians enrolled in Medicare (under §1866(j) of the SSA) and other eligible professionals who participate in the Physician Quality Reporting Initiative (now the Physician Quality Reporting System). The Secretary was required, by January 1, 2013, to implement a plan to make publicly available comparative information on physician performance on quality and patient experience measures (consistent with privacy protections codified at 5 U.S.C.

552 and 552a). This information is required to include, among other things, measures collected under PQRS and an assessment of efficiency, patient health outcomes, and patient experience, as specified. In developing and implementing this plan, the Secretary was required to consider a number of factors, including, among others, processes to ensure appropriate attribution and processes to ensure that data made publicly available are statistically valid and reliable. The Secretary is required to consider the feedback from the multi-stakeholder groups (consistent with §1890(b)(7) and §1890A) when selecting measures for use under this section and must consider the plan to transition to a value-based purchasing program for physicians (under §131 of MIPPA) when developing and implementing the plan under this section. The Secretary is required to report to Congress, not later than January 1, 2015, on the Physician Compare website, as specified; at any time before the submission of this report, the Secretary is authorized to expand the information available on the Physician Compare website to other provider types (under Title XVIII) and to establish, at any time not later than January 1, 2019, a demonstration program to provide financial incentives to Medicare beneficiaries who utilize high-quality physicians (as determined by the Secretary based on information included on the Physician Compare website).

On April 9, 2014, CMS released the Medicare Provider Utilization and Payment Data: Physician and Other Supplier Public Use File, including information about services provided to Medicare beneficiaries by physicians and other health care professionals. The data set contains over 9 million Part B FFS claims with information on utilization, payment (allowed amount and Medicare payment), submitted charges, and place of service, organized for more than 800,000 physicians or other noninstitutional health care providers.

This provision of H.R. 2 would require the Secretary to make publicly available, on an annual basis, information with respect to physicians and other eligible professionals on items and services furnished to Medicare beneficiaries. The information made available under this section would be required to be similar to, and made available in a similar manner to, the information in the Medicare Provider Utilization and Payment Data: Physician and Other Supplier Public Use File. The information made available would be required to include, at a minimum, (1) information on the number of services furnished under Part B; (2) information on submitted charges and payments for services; and (3) a unique identifier for the physician or eligible professional that is available to the public. The information would further be required to be made searchable by at least (1) specialty or type of physician or eligible professional; (2) characteristics of the services furnished (e.g., volume); and (3) the location of the physician or eligible professional. Beginning in 2016, this information would be required to be integrated on the Physician Compare website.

Section 105: Expanding Availability of Medicare Data

Section 105(a), (c), and (d): Expanding Uses of Medicare Data by Qualified Entities

The information contained in Medicare claims is extensive and voluminous, encompassing many decades of historical records and serving as a repository for the comprehensive record of the Medicare experience of both providers and beneficiaries. Researchers, insurers, patient advocates, and others long have argued that the ability to access and analyze Medicare data would lead to a better understanding of our health care delivery system and the ability to improve patient care. Under current law (SSA §1874(e)), certain qualified entities (defined as public or private entities qualified to use claims data to evaluate the performance of providers of services and suppliers on measures of quality, efficiency, effectiveness, and resource use) have access to standard extracts of Parts A, B, and D claims data, subject to some restrictions and limitations.

This provision of H.R. 2 would expand the uses of Medicare data by qualified entities, to the extent consistent with applicable information, privacy, security, and disclosure laws. Beginning July 1, 2016, a qualified entity could use Medicare claims data combined with claims data from other sources in the evaluation of the performance of providers of services and suppliers, to conduct additional nonpublic analyses (as determined appropriate by the Secretary), and to provide or sell such analyses to authorized users for nonpublic use (including for the purposes of assisting providers of services and suppliers to develop and participate in quality and patient care improvement activities, including developing new models of care).

Any analyses provided or sold to an employer could be used only by the employer for purposes of providing health insurance to its employees and retirees. A qualified entity could not provide or sell an analysis to a health insurance issuer unless the issuer is providing the qualified entity with data as part of the combined claims data as mentioned above.

Beginning July 1, 2016, a qualified entity could provide or sell the combined data to a provider of services, a supplier, or a medical society or hospital association for nonpublic use, including for assisting providers of service and suppliers in developing and participating in quality and patient care improvement activities, including developing new models of care.

An analysis or data that is provided or sold as described above could not contain information that individually identifies a patient except in the case of information on patients of the provider of services or supplier itself. An authorized user would be prohibited from using an analysis or data provided or sold as described above for marketing purposes.

A data use agreement would be required of qualified entities and authorized users regarding the use of any data that the qualified entity is providing or selling to the authorized user. The agreement would describe the requirements for privacy and security of the data and, as determined appropriate by the Secretary, any prohibitions on using the data to link to other individually identifiable sources of information. If the authorized user were not a covered entity under the Health Insurance Portability and Accountability Act rules, the agreement would identify the relevant regulations, as determined by the Secretary, with which the user would comply if it were to act in the capacity of a covered entity.

An authorized user that is provided or sold an analysis or data would not redisclose or make public the analysis or data or any analysis using the data, except for the purposes of performance improvement and care coordination activities. Prior to a qualified entity providing or selling an analysis to an authorized user, the qualified entity would provide the provider or supplier with the opportunity to appeal and correct errors.

In the case of a breach of a data use agreement, the Secretary would impose on the qualified entity an assessment of up to $100 for each individual entitled to or enrolled for Medicare Part A or Part B benefits. This would apply both in the case of an agreement between the Secretary and a qualified entity and an agreement between a qualified entity and an authorized user. Any amounts thereby collected would be deposited in Federal Supplementary Medical Insurance Trust Fund.

Any qualified entity that provides or sells an analysis or data as described above would submit an annual report to the Secretary that includes (a) a summary of the analyses provided or sold, including the number of such analyses, the number of purchasers of such analyses, and the total amount of fees received for such analyses; (b) a description of the topics and purposes of such analyses; (c) information on the entities who received the data, the uses of the data, and the total amount of fees received for providing, selling, or sharing the data; and (d) other information determined appropriate by the Secretary.

Beginning July 1, 2016, the provision also would extend the availability of standard data extracts beyond the Medicare program to include Medicaid and the Children's Health Insurance Program (CHIP), as the Secretary determines appropriate. In addition, any fees collected as a result of making this data available would be deposited into the CMS Program Management Account beginning July 1, 2016, instead of the Federal Supplementary Medical Insurance (Part B) Trust Fund.

Section 105(b): Access to Medicare Data by Qualified Clinical Data Registries to Facilitate Quality Improvement

Section 601(b) of the American Taxpayer Relief Act of 2012 (ATRA; P.L. 112-240) (SSA §1848(m)(3)(E)) required the Secretary of Health and Human Services to deem those eligible professionals who satisfactorily participate in a "qualified clinical data registry" as having met the quality reporting requirements for a Physician Quality Reporting System (PQRS) for 2014 and subsequent years. CMS established the PQRS to reward eligible professionals for reporting specified quality data to the agency. The section also required the Secretary to establish requirements for a qualified clinical data registry and, in so doing, to consider, among other things, whether an entity has mechanisms in place to ensure transparency and to support quality improvement initiatives for participants. Measures used in the qualified clinical data registries may be endorsed by the National Quality Forum. These measures are not subject to the process for measure selection being carried out by multi-stakeholder groups under SSA Section 1890A. In defining the requirements for the qualified clinical data registries, the Secretary was required to consult with interested parties and establish a process to determine whether the requirements have been met. GAO was required to conduct a study on the potential of clinical data registries to improve the quality and efficiency of care in the Medicare program, including through payment incentives. As required by statute, GAO submitted a report to Congress on this study in December 2013.[2]

This provision of H.R. 2 would require the Secretary, beginning on July 1, 2016, to provide upon request Medicare claims data and, as the Secretary determines appropriate, Medicaid and CHIP claims data, to qualified clinical data registries. This data would be provided for the purpose of linking it with clinical outcomes data and for performing analyses and research in support of quality improvement activities. The provision would further require that any public reporting of these analyses or research that identifies a provider gives the provider an opportunity to appeal and correct errors, as specified. The provision would require that the data be provided at a fee equal to the cost of providing such data.

Section 106: Reducing Administrative Burden and Other Provisions

Section 106(a): Medicare Physician and Practitioner Opt out to Private Contract

Physicians can furnish health care services to Medicare beneficiaries and receive payment from the Medicare program as either a participating physician or as a nonparticipating physician. Participating physicians sign an agreement (affidavit) to accept Medicare payment rates as payment in full for care provided to Medicare beneficiaries and cannot balance-bill beneficiaries. Nonparticipating physicians can still provide care to Medicare beneficiaries, but they receive Medicare payments for covered services that are 95% of the amount for participating physicians. However, nonparticipating physicians are allowed to balance bill beneficiaries subject to certain limits. The balance billing limit is 115% of the fee schedule amount for nonparticipating physicians, which works out to 9.25% higher than the amount recognized for participating physicians (i.e., $1.15 \times 0.95 = 1.0925$).

Alternatively, beginning in 1998, physicians and certain practitioners can enter into private contracts (under SSA §1861(r)) with Medicare Part B beneficiaries, provide services, and bill patients without being subject to the upper payment limits specified by Medicare. *Opting out* is available to physicians, including doctors of medicine and osteopathy, dentists, podiatrists, optometrists; physician assistants, nurse practitioners, and clinical nurse specialists; certified registered nurse anesthetists; certified nurse midwives; clinical psychologists; clinical social workers; and registered dieticians and nutrition professionals. Physical and occupational therapists in independent practice and chiropractors are not allowed to opt out. However, if and when a physician/practitioner decides to enter a private contract with a Medicare patient, that physician/practitioner must agree to forego any reimbursement by Medicare for all Medicare beneficiaries for two years. In the case of emergency or urgent care, Medicare will pay for services provided by an opt out physician/practitioner to a beneficiary with whom they have not signed an opt-out agreement.

The patient is not subject to the two-year limit; the patient would continue to be able to see other physicians who were not private contracting physicians and have Medicare pay for the services. A private contract is unnecessary, and private contracting rules do not apply for non-covered services (e.g., cosmetic surgery); there are no limits on what may be charged for non-covered service.

This provision of H.R. 2 would permit automatic extensions of private contracts unless the physician or practitioner provides a notice of non-extension not later than 30 days before the end of the period. This policy would be effective for affidavits signed on or after 60 days of enactment. The Secretary of HHS would be required to make certain information on providers and practitioners in private contracts publicly available. No later than February 1, 2016, the Secretary would make information on the number and characteristics of opt-out physicians and practitioners publicly available through a public HHS website and update the information annually. At a minimum, the website would include information about the opt-out physicians' and practitioners' (1) number, (2) professional specialty or other designation, (3) geographic distribution, (4) timing regarding becoming opt-out physicians and practitioners, relative to when they first enrolled in the Medicare program and with respect to applicable two-year periods, and (5) proportion (of opt-out physicians and practitioners) who billed for emergency or urgent care services.

Section 106(b): Promoting Interoperability of Electronic Health Record Systems

The Health Information Technology for Economic and Clinical Health (HITECH) Act of 2009 amended Medicare (i.e., SSA §§1814(l)(3), 1848(o), 1853(l) and (m), and 1886(n)) and Medicaid (i.e., SSA §1903(a)(3)(F) and (t)) to authorize incentive payments to eligible hospitals and physicians—and certain other health care professionals—who attest to being "meaningful users" of certified electronic health record (EHR) technology. The HITECH Act defined meaningful use as using certified EHR technology in a meaningful manner (e.g., e-prescribing) and using the technology to exchange electronic health information with another EHR system and to report clinical quality measures to the Secretary. The law also instructed the Secretary to make the measures of meaningful use more stringent over time, which CMS is doing in stages.

To meet the initial stage (i.e., Stage 1) of meaningful use, eligible hospitals and physicians must use their EHR technology to meet a series of objectives that generally involve capturing and storing structured patient data (e.g., vital signs, medications, lab test results). Providers must use EHR technology that has been certified by an accredited certification authority to perform these functions. Providers now in their third or fourth year of participation in the program are moving to meaningful use Stage 2, under which they must use their EHR technology to perform certain additional functions including some exchange of patient data during transitions of care (e.g., a hospital discharge to a rehabilitation facility, or a physician referral). The term EHR interoperability is used to refer to the ability of EHR systems not just to exchange electronic information but to be able to use the information based on common standards. Although the Medicare and Medicaid incentive programs have had a significant impact on promoting the widespread adoption and use of EHR technology in hospitals and physician practices across the country, significant challenges remain in achieving widespread EHR interoperability.

This provision of H.R. 2 would declare it a national objective to achieve widespread interoperability of certified EHR technology by December 31, 2018. The Secretary would be required, in consultation with stakeholders, by July 1, 2016, to establish interoperability metrics to measure progress towards achieving that objective. If the objective were not met by December 31, 2018, then the Secretary would have until December 31, 2019, to submit a report to Congress identifying the barriers to widespread interoperability and providing recommendations for achieving the objective. Such recommendations may include (1) payment adjustments for not being meaningful EHR users under the Medicare EHR incentive program; and (2) the criteria for decertifying certified EHR technology products.

The Medicare EHR incentive program would be amended to require eligible hospitals and physicians, beginning one year after enactment, to indicate through meaningful use attestation (or some other process specified by the Secretary) that they had not knowingly and willfully taken any action to limit or restrict the interoperability of their certified EHR technology.

The Secretary would be required, within one year of enactment, to submit to Congress a report on ways to help providers compare and select certified EHR technology, such as through surveying EHR users and vendors and making such information publicly available.

Section 106(c): GAO Studies and Reports on the Use of Telehealth Under Federal Programs and on Remote Patient Monitoring Services

Section 1834(m) of the SSA authorizes Medicare reimbursement to physicians for telehealth services provided via live video conferencing. Such reimbursement is limited to certain types of services provided, mostly consultations, psychological counseling and screenings, and pharmacologic management. The services must be provided to an eligible Medicare beneficiary in an eligible facility (e.g., physician office, hospital, health center, or rural health clinic) located outside of a Metropolitan Statistical Area. Medicare reimbursement for telehealth services totaled $12 million in 2013.

This provision of H.R. 2 would require the GAO, within two years of enactment, to submit two reports to Congress, each with recommendations for legislative and administrative actions. GAO would be permitted to combine both reports into a single document. The first report, focused on the Medicare telehealth program, would examine and evaluate (1) how the various definitions of telehealth used in federal programs can inform the use of telehealth under Medicare; (2) factors that can facilitate or inhibit the use of telehealth under Medicare; and (3) the potential implications of expanding telehealth in the transformation of payment and delivery systems under Medicare (and Medicaid); and (4) how CMS monitors Medicare telehealth payments.

The second report, focused on remote patient monitoring technology and services, would examine and evaluate (1) the private health insurance incentives for adopting such technology; (2) the patients, conditions, and clinical circumstances that could most benefit from using such services; (3) the barriers to adopting such services under Medicare; and (4) the challenges in placing a value on remote patient monitoring services under the Medicare PFS in order to reflect accurately the resources involved in furnishing such services.

Section 106(d): Rule of Construction Regarding Health Care Providers

This provision of H.R. 2 would provide that the development, recognition, or implementation of any guideline or standard under the ACA, Medicare, or Medicaid cannot be construed to establish the standard of care or duty of care owed by a health care provider to a patient in any medical malpractice or medical product liability action or claim. However, this provision would not preempt any state or common law governing medical professional or medical product liability actions or claims.

Title II—Medicare and Other Health Extenders

Subtitle A. Medicare Extenders

Section 201: Extension of Work Geographic Practice Cost Indices Floor

The Medicare physician fee schedule is adjusted geographically for three factors to reflect differences in the cost of resources needed to produce physician services: physician work, practice expense, and medical malpractice insurance. The geographic adjustments are indices— known as Geographic Practice Cost Indices (GPCIs)—that reflect how each area compares to the national average in a "market basket" of goods. A value of 1.00 represents the average across all areas. These indices are used in the calculation of the payment rate under the Medicare physician fee schedule. A series of bills set a temporary floor value of 1.00 on the physician work index beginning in January 2004 and continuing through March 31, 2015.

This provision of H.R. 2 extends the 1.00 floor for the physician work geographic index through December 31, 2017.

Section 202: Extension of Therapy Cap Exceptions Process

Medicare beneficiaries face two annual payment limits for all Medicare-covered outpatient therapy services. Established by BBA97, these limits initially applied to therapy services provided by *nonhospital providers,* to be applied separately for (1) physical therapy services and speech-language pathology services, and (2) occupational therapy services. Initially set at $1,500 to apply beginning in 1999, these limits were suspended from 2000 to 2005. The Deficit Reduction Act of 2005 (DRA; P.L. 109-171) reimplemented the limits beginning in 2006 and required the Secretary to implement an exceptions process for services meeting specified criteria for medically necessary services. A series of legislative acts have extended the exceptions process, increased the limits, and modified the conditions for the application of the caps each year since.

The Middle Class Tax Relief and Job Creation Act of 2012 (MCTRJCA; P.L. 112-96) set the annual threshold at $3,700, to be applied separately for the two categories of therapy services effective October 1, 2012. However, this increased amount applied to therapy services received both in physicians' offices *and* in hospital outpatient departments for the first time. ATRA extended the application of the cap and threshold to therapy services furnished in a hospital outpatient department and in a critical access hospital (CAH). ATRA also extended the mandate that Medicare perform manual medical review of therapy services for which an exception is requested when the beneficiary has reached a dollar aggregate threshold amount of $3,700 for therapy services. PSRA and PAMA extended the therapy cap exceptions process through March 31, 2015.

This provision in H.R. 2 would extend the exceptions process through December 31, 2017, and require the Secretary to implement a new medical review process for outpatient therapy services. In determining which therapy services to review, the Secretary could identify services furnished by a therapy provider who (1) has had a high claims-denial percentage or is less compliant with applicable Medicare program requirements; (2) has a pattern of billing for therapy services that is aberrant compared to peers or otherwise has questionable billing practices, such as billing medically unlikely units of services in a day; (3) is newly enrolled or has not previously furnished therapy services under the Medicare program; (4) provides services to treat a type of medical condition; or (5) is part of a group that includes another therapy provider identified by the preceding factors.

To implement this new medical review process, CMS would receive $5 million from the Federal Supplementary Medical Insurance (Medicare Part B) Trust Fund for FY2015 and FY2016, to remain available until expended. These funds could not be used by a Medicare recovery audit contractor (RAC) for medical reviews of therapy services.

Section 203: Extension of Ambulance Add-Ons

The SSA provides for bonus payments for ground ambulance services that originate in qualified rural areas (called *super rural areas*) furnished on or after July 1, 2004, and before April 1, 2015. The super rural areas are those counties with the lowest population densities that collectively represent 25% of the total population. CMS estimated and set the super rural bonus as a 22.6% increase in the base rate for the transport. Subsequently, the Medicare rates for ground ambulance services otherwise established for the year were increased an additional 3% for rural ambulance services and 2% for urban ambulance services before April 1, 2015.

H.R. 2 would extend the super rural, rural, and urban add-ons to Medicare's ambulance fee schedule until January 1, 2018.

Section 204: Extension of Increased Inpatient Hospital Payment Adjustment for Certain Low-Volume Hospitals

Under the Medicare Inpatient Prospective Payment System (IPPS), qualifying hospitals receive increased payments to account for the higher incremental costs associated with a low volume of discharges. The Secretary is required to determine an empirically appropriate percentage increase per discharge, up to a ceiling of 25%, for low-volume hospitals more than 25 road miles from a comparable hospital. These hospitals could have as many as 800 *total* discharges. CMS determined that hospitals with fewer than 200 *total* (Medicare and non-Medicare) discharges located more than 25 road miles from another acute care hospital qualified for a 25% increase. The ACA temporarily relaxed the requirements for hospitals to receive increased low-volume payments, starting for discharges in FY2011. The low volume standards were changed from no more than 800 *total* discharges and no comparable hospital closer than 25 road miles to no more than 1,600 total *Medicare* discharges and no comparable hospital closer than 15 road miles. Qualifying hospitals with 200 or fewer Medicare discharges receive a payment increase of 25% per discharge, which diminishes to no increase for hospitals with 1,600 Medicare discharges. The low-volume adjustment will revert to the original, more stringent standards (no more than 800 total discharges, more than 25 road miles, a flat 25% increase) starting for discharges on April 1, 2015.

H.R. 2 would extend the more generous low-volume adjustment standards until October 1, 2017.

Section 205: Extension of the Medicare-Dependent Hospital Program

Medicare-dependent hospitals (MDHs) are small, rural hospitals with a high proportion of patients who are Medicare beneficiaries. Specifically, MDHs have no more than 100 beds and at least 60% of acute inpatient days or discharges attributable to Medicare in FY1987 or in two of the three most recently audited cost reporting periods. MDHs receive special treatment, including higher payments, under Medicare's IPPS. The MDH special payment status will expire by April 1, 2015.

H.R. 2 would extend the MDH program until October 1, 2017, and would make other technical conforming changes.

Section 206: Extension for Specialized Medicare Advantage Plans for Special Needs Individuals

The Medicare Prescription Drug, Improvement, and Modernization Act of 2003 (MMA; P.L. 108-173) established a new type of Medicare Advantage (MA) coordinated care plan focused on individuals with special needs. Special needs plans (SNPs) are allowed to target enrollment to one or more types of special needs individuals, including those who are (1) institutionalized, (2) dually eligible, or (3) living with severe or disabling chronic conditions. Among other changes, ACA Section 3205 extended SNP authority through December 31, 2013, and temporarily extended authority through the end of 2012 for SNPs that do not have contracts with state Medicaid programs to continue to operate, but not to expand their service area.

ATRA extended SNP authority to operate through December 31, 2014, and also temporarily authorized SNPs without contracts with state Medicaid programs to continue to operate but not to expand their service areas. PSRA temporarily extended SNP authority through December 31, 2015. PAMA temporarily extended SNP authority through December 31, 2016.

This provision of H.R. 2 would extend SNP authority to operate for two additional years through December 31, 2018.

Section 207: Extension of Funding for Quality Measure Endorsement, Input, and Selection

Section 183 of the Medicare Improvements for Patients and Providers Act of 2008 (MIPPA) (SSA §1890) required the Secretary of HHS to have a contract with a consensus-based entity (e.g., National Quality Forum, or NQF) to carry out specified duties related to performance improvement and measurement. These duties include, among others, priority setting; measure endorsement; measure maintenance; convening multi-stakeholder groups to provide input on the selection of quality measures and national priorities; and annual reporting to Congress. Section 183 of MIPPA required the Secretary to provide for the transfer of $10 million for each of FY2009 through FY2012 from the Medicare Part A and B Trust Funds to carry out the activities under Section 1890 of the SSA. Section 609 of ATRA extended this funding through FY2013.

Section 3014(b) of the ACA required the Secretary to establish a pre-rulemaking process to select quality measures for use under Title XVIII (SSA §1890A(a)-(d)). This process includes gathering multi-stakeholder input; making measures under consideration available to the public; transmission to, and consideration by, the Secretary of the input of multi-stakeholder groups;

and publication of the rationale for the use of any quality measure in the *Federal Register*; among others. The Secretary is required to establish a process for disseminating quality measures used by the Secretary; the Secretary also is required to review quality measures periodically and determine whether to maintain the use of a measure or to phase it out. In addition, ACA Section 3014(a) adds new duties for the consensus-based entity under the contract in SSA Section 1890 (multi-stakeholder group convening and reporting duties). Through its Measure Applications Partnership (MAP), NQF has been convening multi-stakeholder groups to provide input into the selection of quality measures for use in the Medicare and other federal health programs; MAP publishes annual reports with recommendations for selection of quality measures in February of each year. Section 3014(c) of the ACA provided for the transfer of $20 million for each of FY2010 through FY2014 from the Medicare Part A and B Trust Funds for these activities.

Section 109 of PAMA required the transfer of $5 million for FY2014 and $15 million for the first six months of FY2015 from the Medicare Part A and B Trust Funds to carry out both Section 1890 and Section 1890A(a)-(d) of the SSA; funds are required to remain available until expended.

This provision of H.R. 2 would strike the language in PAMA providing for $15 million for the first six months of FY2015 and replace it with language that would provide for the transfer of $30 million for each of FY2015 through FY2017 from the Medicare Part A and B Trust Funds to carry out the activities under SSA Section 1890 and SSA Section 1890A(a)-(d). These funds are required to remain available until expended.

Section 208: Extension of Funding Outreach and Assistance for Low-Income Programs

Section 119 of MIPPA appropriated $25 million for FY2008 and FY2009 for low-income Medicare beneficiary outreach and education activities through the following programs: State Health Insurance Assistance Programs (SHIPs), Area Agencies on Aging (AAAs), Aging and Disability Resource Centers (ADRCs), and the Administration on Aging (AoA). Section 3306 of the ACA extended these programs and appropriated a total of $45 million for FY2010 through FY2012 for these and other programs such as Medicare Part D low income subsidy outreach and the Medicare Savings Program.

ATRA extended MIPPA Section 119 authorities through FY2013 and appropriated a total of $25 million in the following amounts for low-income Medicare beneficiary outreach and assistance programs: SHIPs, $7.5 million;

AAAs, $7.5 million; ADRCs, $5 million; and the Contract with the National Center for Benefits and Outreach Enrollment, $5 million.

The Pathway for SGR Reform Act of 2013 (PSRA) extended MIPPA Section 119 authorities through the second quarter of FY2014 (March 31, 2014) and appropriated funding at FY2013 funding levels prorated for the first two quarters of FY2014 (i.e., PSRA appropriated half a year's worth of FY2014 funding).

PAMA extended MIPPA Section 119 authorities through the second quarter of FY2015 (March 31, 2015). For FY2014, it provided a total of $25 million in funding for low-income Medicare beneficiary outreach and assistance programs at FY2013 funding levels: SHIPs, $7.5 million; AAAs, $7.5 million; ADRCs, $5.0 million; and the Contract with the National Center for Benefits and Outreach Enrollment, $5.0 million. In addition, PAMA appropriated funding at FY2014 funding levels prorated for the first two quarters of FY2015 (i.e., PAMA appropriated half a year's worth of FY2015 funding).

Table 1. H.R. 2, Section 208: Low-Income Outreach and Assistance Programs Appropriations (FY2015 through FY2017)

Low-Income	FY2015	FY2016	FY2017
Program/Appropriations	Appropriations	Appropriations	Appropriations
State Health Insurance Assistance	$7.5 million	$13 million	$13 million
Programs (SHIPs)			
Area Agencies on Aging (AAAs)	$7.5 million	$7.5 million	$7.5 million
Aging and Disability Resource Centers (ADRCs)	$5.0 million	$5.0 million	$5.0 million
Contract with the National Center for Benefits and Outreach	$5.0 million	$12.0 million	$12.0 million
Enrollment			
Total	$25 million	$37.5 million	$37.5 million

Source: Congressional Research Service summary of Section 208 of H.R. 2, the Medicare Access and CHIP Reauthorization Act of 2015.

H.R. 2 would extend MIPPA Section 119 authorities through FY2017. For FY2015, it would provide a total of $25 million in funding at the previous year's funding levels, as shown in Table 1. For each of FY2016 and FY2017, it would appropriate a total of $37.5 million for low-income Medicare beneficiary outreach and assistance programs, a $12.5 million increase from FY2015 funding levels. It would increase funding for SHIPs by $5.5 million and the Contract with the National Center for Benefits and Outreach Enrollment by $7 million for each of FY2016 and FY2017.

Section 209: Extension and Transition of Reasonable Cost Reimbursement Contracts

Reasonable cost plans (or cost plans) are Medicare managed care plans that are reimbursed by Medicare for the actual cost of providing services to enrollees. Cost plans were created in the Tax Equity and Fiscal Responsibility Act of 1982 (TEFRA; P.L. 97-248). BBA97 included a provision to phase out the reasonable cost contracts, however, the phaseout has been delayed over the years through congressional action. After January 1, 2016, the Secretary cannot extend or renew a cost contract for a service area if (1) during the entire previous year there were either two or more Medicare Advantage (MA) regional plans or two or more MA local plans in the service area offered by different MA organizations, and (2) these regional or local plans met specified minimum enrollment requirements.

In contrast to reasonable cost plans, MA plans under Medicare Part C are paid a capitated monthly payment for each beneficiary enrolled in their plan regardless of the actual cost of providing required services to each enrollee. The plan is at risk if costs for all of its enrollees exceed program payments and beneficiary cost sharing; conversely, in general, the plan can retain savings if aggregate enrollee costs are less than program payments and cost sharing.

The per-beneficiary payment under MA is determined by comparing a plan's bid to a benchmark. A bid is the plan's estimated cost of providing Medicare-covered services (excluding hospice but including the cost of medical services, administration, and profit). A benchmark is the maximum amount the federal government will pay for providing those services in the plan's service area. If a plan's bid is less than the benchmark, its payment equals its bid plus a rebate equal to the difference between the bid and the benchmark. If a plan's bid is equal to or above the benchmark, its payment equals the benchmark amount and each enrollee in that plan will pay an additional premium that is equal to the amount by which the bid exceeds the benchmark. Benchmarks are adjusted based on plan quality such that a plan with 4 or 5 stars on a 5-star quality rating scale receives a 5 percentage point increase in its benchmark. Plans that are new (and do not have data upon which to base a quality rating) or have low enrollment receive a 3.5 percentage point increase in their benchmark.

H.R. 2 would transition reasonable cost plans that can no longer qualify to be cost plans under the current statutory requirements into Medicare Advantage plans. It would also allow cost plans that would otherwise qualify under the statutory requirement to voluntarily transition into MA plans.

The following five provisions of H.R. 2 would apply if (a) a reasonable cost contract plan could not be renewed because, during the previous year, the plan's service area also was served by two or more MA regional or two or more MA local plans that met specific enrollment requirements, or (b) an organization with a reasonable cost contract voluntarily sought not to renew its contract, but rather to convert it to an MA plan.

- The contract may be extended for the two years subsequent to 2016. The contract's final year is referred to as the "last reasonable cost reimbursement contract year for the contract" or the "last year."
- The organization would be prohibited from enrolling new beneficiaries during the last year, and new enrollment during the prior year would be restricted. Beneficiaries would not be allowed to enroll in the cost plan during the annual election period that applied to the last year. A beneficiary whose spouse was an enrollee under the cost contract would not be able to enroll in the cost plan during the year prior to the last year. A beneficiary who was covered by an employer group health plan offered through the cost contract also would be prohibited from enrolling in the cost plan in the year prior to the last year. In addition, beneficiaries who become eligible for Medicare and, just prior to Medicare eligibility, were enrolled in a non-Medicare plan offered by the organization would not be able to enroll in the cost plan for the year prior to the last year.
- The organization offering the cost plan would be required to notify the Secretary whether or not the contract was to be converted, in whole or in part, to an MA plan for the year following the last year.
- If the organization were to convert the cost plan to an MA plan, the organization would be required to provide the Secretary with the information necessary to carry out the deeming enrollment process (described below) and the bidding review process used to determine MA payments.
- If a cost plan enrolls a beneficiary during the last year, the organization would be required to notify the individual that it was the

> last year for the contract. During the last year and the year prior to the last year, the organization would be permitted to offer an MA plan in the same area and would be allowed to enroll beneficiaries in both the MA plan and the cost plan.

If an organization offering a cost plan informs the Secretary that it will be converted to an MA plan, enrollees would be deemed to enroll in the new MA plan under certain circumstances. A beneficiary who was enrolled in a cost plan during the last year of a reasonable cost contract is deemed to elect to receive benefits through an applicable MA plan, unless he or she elects otherwise, but only if certain provisions apply. First, the beneficiary would have to have been enrolled in the reasonable cost plan in the previous year, and the plan would have had to have been extended or renewed for the last year. Second, the cost plan would have had to provide notice to the enrollee that it was to be converted to an MA plan. Third, the applicable MA plan would have to have been, in fact, converted from a cost plan and offered by the same entity or organization that had previously entered into the cost contract, and in the same service area.

Fourth, the premiums and other costs determined by the Secretary for both the cost plan and the subsequent MA plan would not be allowed to exceed a threshold established by the Secretary.

The subsequent MA plan would be required to maintain networks of providers and suppliers, and courses of treatment for beneficiaries currently in care for at least 90 days after the conversion to help enrollees with the transition. During the 90-day transition, the MA plan would be required to pay providers and suppliers amounts that were not less than what is paid under original Medicare. Beneficiaries who are eligible for the deemed enrollment process and did not have drug coverage in their reasonable cost plans would be enrolled in a MA plan without a Part D drug benefit. Beneficiaries that had drug coverage under a cost plan would be enrolled in a MA plan with Part D coverage. The Secretary would be required to identify and notify the enrollees affected by the deemed enrollment process no later than 45 days before the first day of the annual, coordinated election period for the plan year beginning on or after January 1, 2017.

H.R. 2 would create a special election period for beneficiaries who were deemed to enroll in a newly converted MA plan or a Medicare Advantage prescription drug (MA-PD) plan. The special election period would last from after the last day of the annual coordinated election period (December 8) until the end of February of the first plan year for which the beneficiary is enrolled in the MA plan. Eligible beneficiaries would be able to change their plan selection during that time, including changing from an MA plan to an MA-PD plan or from an MA-PD plan to an MA plan. However, the beneficiary would be able to exercise this option only once. A beneficiary who developed end-stage renal disease while enrolled in a cost contract that converted to an MA contract would be eligible for the deemed enrollment process as well.

H.R. 2 would require an MA organization offering a newly converted MA plan to provide enrollees with the following information: (1) a notification that the individual will be deemed to have made an election to receive benefits under an MA plan or an MA-PD plan for the next year, but that the individual may make a different election during the annual, coordinated election period, (2) the information that the Secretary is required to send to all beneficiaries prior to the beginning of the annual, coordinated election period, (3) a description of the differences between an MA plan or an MA-PD plan and the reasonable cost plan in which the individual was recently enrolled, including information on benefits, cost sharing, premiums, drug coverage, and provider networks, (4) information about special election periods, and (5) other information the Secretary may specify.

With respect to any quality adjustments applied to the newly converted plan's MA benchmark, for the first three years after a cost plan converts to an MA plan, H.R. 2 would require that the plan would not be treated as a new MA plan. Rather, the star rating for the converted MA plan would be determined based on available data. To the extent that data is not available, the Secretary would be required to use data from a period during which the plan was still a reasonable cost plan.

Section 210: Extension of Home Health Rural Add-On

As required by Congress, Medicare provides increased payments under the home health prospective payment system (HH PPS) for home health care provided to beneficiaries in rural areas. The Benefits Improvement and Protection Act of 2000 (BIPA; P.L. 106-554) established a 10% increase to Medicare's HH PPS rates for home health care provided to beneficiaries in rural areas beginning April 1, 2001, through March 31, 2003. The MMA reestablished this rural add-on at a 5% increase beginning April 1, 2004, through March 31, 2005. DRA reestablished the 5% rural add-on beginning January 1, 2006, through December 31, 2006. ACA reestablished the rural add-on at a 3% increase beginning April 1, 2010, through December 31, 2015.

H.R. 2 would extend the rural add-on under the HH PPS at a 3% increase for home health care provided to beneficiaries in rural areas from January 1, 2016, through December 31, 2017.

Subtitle B. Other Health Extenders

Section 211: Permanent Extension of the Qualifying Individual Program

BBA97 required states to pay Medicare Part B premiums for a new group of low-income Medicare beneficiaries—qualifying individuals (QIs)—whose income was between 120% and 135% of the federal poverty level (FPL). BBA97 also amended SSA to provide for Medicaid payment for QIs through an annual transfer from the Medicare Part B Trust Fund to be allocated to states. States (and the District of Columbia) receive 100% federal funding to pay QIs' Medicare premiums up to the federal allocation, but they receive no additional matching beyond the annual allocation. In September 2014, approximately 499,700 low-income Medicare beneficiaries received financial assistance from state Medicaid programs to pay their Part B premiums. The QI program has been reauthorized and funded a number of times since it was established by BBA97. Most recently, Section 201 of PAMA reauthorized the QI program through March 31, 2015, and appropriated $1.035 billion in funding.

This provision of H.R. 2 would permanently extend the QI program and appropriate $535 million for the remainder of CY2015 (April 1, 2015-December 31, 2015) and $980 million for CY2016. The amount of funding for CY2017 and subsequent calendar years would be determined by the product of the following: (1) the previous year's QI allocation, (2) the increase from the previous year in Medicare Part B premium, and (3) the estimated increase from the previous year in Part B enrollment.

Section 212: Permanent Extension of Transitional Medical Assistance

Medicaid requires states to continue Medicaid benefits for certain low-income families that otherwise would lose coverage because of changes in income. This continuation is known as transitional medical assistance (TMA). States must provide TMA to families losing eligibility based on Section 1931 of the SSA under two scenarios. First, states were permanently required to provide four months of TMA coverage to families who lose Medicaid eligibility under Section 1931 due to increased child *or* spousal support collections. At state option, families eligible for this four-month extension must have been receiving Medicaid under Section 1931 in at least three of the preceding six months.[3] The four-month extension of coverage for individuals losing eligibility due to increased spousal support does not have a sunset date. However, with the transition to the modified adjusted gross income (MAGI) income counting rules by January 1, 2014, the extension of eligibility for individuals losing coverage under Section 1931 due to increased child support is no longer relevant, as child support is not counted as income under MAGI-based income counting methodologies.

Second, under Section 1902(e)(1) and Section 1925, states are required to provide TMA to families losing Section 1931 Medicaid eligibility for work-related reasons (otherwise referred to as work-related TMA). States originally were required to provide four months of TMA to families losing eligibility due to an increase in hours of work or income from employment. However, the Family Support Act (FSA) of 1988 (P.L. 100-485) expanded state TMA requirements under Section 1925, requiring states to provide at least 6, and up to 12, months of TMA to families losing Section 1931 Medicaid eligibility due to increased hours of work or income from employment, as well as to families that lose eligibility due to the loss of a time-limited earned income disregard that allows families to qualify for Medicaid at higher income levels for a set period of time. States are given the option of meeting this requirement by using Medicaid funds to pay for a family's premiums or other related costs for employer-based coverage when available. After the initial six-month period, families may continue coverage for an additional six months if the family's earnings, minus child care costs, do not exceed 185% of the federal poverty level, among other requirements.[4] Additionally, in the second six-month period, states may require families with incomes at or above 100% FPL to pay a premium for the additional coverage. ARRA created an additional work-related TMA option, allowing states to provide work-related TMA for a full 12-month period rather than 2 consecutive 6-month periods.

The FSA originally authorized Section 1925 to replace the four-month requirement in Section 1902(e)(1) through FY1998. The welfare reform law of 1996 (P.L. 104-193) extended Section 1925 thorough FY2001, and the provision has continued to exist under a series of short-term extensions (most recently, through March 31, 2015).

H.R. 2 would extend Section 1925 work-related TMA permanently, requiring states to provide at least 6, and up to 12, months of TMA coverage to families losing Section 1931 Medicaid eligibility due to increased hours of work or income from employment, as well as to families that lose eligibility due to the loss of a time-limited earned income disregard. The provision would not impact the four-month TMA coverage for individuals losing eligibility due to increased spousal support.

Section 213: Extension of Special Diabetes Program for Type I Diabetes and for Indians

BBA97 authorized two diabetes-related programs through the PHSA. The first, authorized in PHSA Section 330B, provides funding for the National Institutes of Health[5] to award grants for research into the prevention and cure of Type I diabetes. The second, authorized in PHSA Section 330C, provides funding for the Indian Health Service (IHS)[6] to award grants for services related to the prevention and treatment of diabetes for American Indians and Alaska Natives who receive services at IHS-funded facilities.[7] BBA97 appropriated funding for both programs from FY1998 through FY2002; subsequent legislation extended funding years and increased amounts appropriated. The programs' most recent extension was in PAMA, which provided $150 million for FY2015 for each program.

This provision of H.R. 2 would extend the annual appropriation of $150 million for each program for each of FY2016 and FY2017.

Section 214: Extension of Abstinence Education

Section 912 of the Personal Responsibility and Work Opportunity Act of 1996 (PRWORA; P.L. 104-193) authorized abstinence education formula grants in Section 510 of the SSA.[8] To receive these formula grants, states must request funding when applying for Maternal and Child Health Block Grant funds[9] authorized in SSA Section 501. Funds provided must be used exclusively for teaching abstinence from sexual activity outside of marriage. PRWORA authorized and appropriated $250 million ($50 million for each of FY1998 through FY2002) for abstinence education. Subsequently, funding for this program was extended through June 30, 2009, by a series of legislation detailed below. ACA Section 2954 appropriated $50 million for each of FY2010 through FY2014 for this program. Most recently, PAMA Section 205 extended funding for the program through FY2015. This program is administered by the Administration for Children and Families (ACF). In addition, several appropriation laws included an additional $5 million for competitive grants for abstinence-only education for each of FY2012, FY2013, FY2014, and FY2015 (P.L. 112-74, P.L. 113-6, P.L. 113-76, and P.L. 113-164/P.L. 113-235, respectively). The funding designated for abstinence education grants expires September 30, 2015.

H.R. 2 would increase and extend funding for Section 510 Abstinence Education grants to $75 million for each of fiscal years 2016 and 2017.

Section 215: Extension of Personal Responsibility Education Program

Section 2953 of the ACA established the Personal Responsibility Education Program (PREP) in Section 513 of the SSA. PREP is a state formula grant program to support evidence-based programs designed to educate adolescents about abstinence, contraception, and adulthood. The ACA also required the Secretary of Health and Human Services to award grants to implement innovative youth pregnancy prevention strategies and to target services to high-risk populations. The ACA (§2953) appropriated a total of $375 million with $75 million appropriated for each of FY2010 through FY2014. The ACA required that $10 million each year be reserved for the youth pregnancy prevention grants. PAMA (§206) extended funding for the program through FY2015. The funds are available until expended. The program is administered by ACF. The funding designated for PREP expires September 30, 2015.

H.R. 2 would extend funding for PREP through FY2017 at $75 million per year.

Section 216: Extension of Funding for Family-to-Family Health Information Centers

The Family-to-Family Health Information Centers program, administered by the Health Resources and Services Administration (HRSA), provides grants to family-staffed organizations that provide health care information and resources to families of children with special health care needs. ACA Section 5507 appropriated $5 million for each of FY2009-FY2012 for Family-to-Family Health Information Centers. ATRA subsequently extended this appropriation an additional year, through FY2013. P.L. 113-67 provided a half year of funding ($2.5 million) for this program that expired April 1, 2014. PAMA provided $2.5 million for the remainder of FY2014 (from April 1 to September 30, 2014) and provided $2.5 million for the first half of FY2015 (October 1, 2014, through March 31, 2015).

This provision of H.R. 2 would strike the partial funding provided in PAMA and provide full-year funding of $5 million for FY2015. It also would provide $5 million for each of FY2016 and FY2017.

Section 217: Extension of Health Workforce Demonstration Project for Low-Income Individuals

Section 5507(a) of the ACA required the Secretary to establish a demonstration project in SSA Section 2008 that awarded funds to states, Indian tribes, institutions of higher education, and local workforce investment boards for health profession opportunity grants (HPOG). These grants were used to help low-income individuals—including individuals receiving assistance from State Temporary Assistance for Needy Families (TANF) programs—to obtain education and training in health care jobs that pay well and are in high demand. Funds also were used to provide financial aid and other supportive services. This program is administered jointly by the HRSA and the Administration for Children and Families (ACF). The ACA appropriated $85 million for HPOG in each of FY2010 through FY2014 ($425 million total), but it reserved a total of $15 million for a demonstration project for personal and home care aides. PAMA provided $85 million for HPOG for FY2015.

This provision of H.R. 2 would extend the HPOG appropriation of $85 million for each of FY2016 and FY2017.

Section 218: Extension of Maternal, Infant, and Early Childhood Home Visiting Programs

Section 2951 of the ACA established the Maternal, Infant, and Early Childhood Home Visiting (MIECHV) program in SSA Section 511.[10] This program provides grants to states, territories, and tribes for the support of evidence-based early childhood home visiting programs. These programs support in-home visits by health or social service professionals with at-risk families. The ACA appropriated a total of $1.45 billion for FY2010 through FY2014 for the program: $100 million for FY2010, $200 million for FY2011, $350 million for FY2012, $400 million for FY2013, and $400 million for FY2014. Of the amount appropriated for this program, 3% annually is reserved for research and evaluation and 3% annually is reserved to make grants to tribal entities for home visitation services to Indian families. This program is administered by the HRSA and the ACF, both at HHS.

PAMA provided $400 million for the MIECHV program for the first half of FY2015 (October 1, 2014, through March 31, 2015). It also reserved portions of this partial-year funding for Indian tribal entities (3% of the appropriation) and research and evaluation (3% of the appropriation).

H.R. 2 would extend the $400 million made available under PAMA through all of FY2015 (October 1, 2014, through September 30, 2015). It also would provide $400 million for each of FY2016 and FY2017.

Section 219: Tennessee Disproportionate Share Hospital Allotment for FY2015- FY2025

The Medicaid statute requires states to make disproportionate share hospital (DSH) payments to hospitals treating large numbers of low-income patients.[11] Although most federal Medicaid funding is provided on an open-ended basis, federal DSH funding is capped. Each state receives an annual DSH allotment, which is the maximum amount of federal matching funds a state is permitted to claim for Medicaid DSH payments. States' Medicaid DSH allotments are based on each state's prior year DSH allotment, but Hawaii and Tennessee have special statutory arrangements for the determination of their respective DSH allotments provided through multiple laws. Most recently, the ACA provided Hawaii a Medicaid DSH allotment for FY2012 and subsequent years, while the Tennessee provision provided an allotment for FY2012 and FY2013. Under current law, Tennessee is the only state without a Medicaid DSH allotment for FY2014 and subsequent years.

This provision would provide a Medicaid DSH allotment to Tennessee in the amount of $53.1 million for each fiscal year from FY2015 through FY2025.

Section 220: Delay in Effective Date for Medicaid Amendments Relating to Beneficiary Liability Settlements

Under third-party liability (TPL) rules, Medicaid is the payer of last resort. If another insurer or payer has financial responsibility for medical services provided to Medicaid beneficiaries, generally that third party is required to pay all or part of the bill before Medicaid pays. Under federal Medicaid law applicable to TPL, states are required to determine if third parties exist and to ensure that providers bill third parties first, before billing Medicaid. DRA strengthened Medicaid TPL by clarifying what entities are considered third parties and requiring states to pass laws that stipulate third parties comply with federal Medicaid TPL law.

States also are required under federal Medicaid TPL law to recover from judgments awarded to Medicaid beneficiaries. For example, if an individual receives medical care following an accident for which Medicaid paid, and the individual later wins a judgment against a third party responsible for that accident (for instance another driver's auto insurance), the state must recover the amount Medicaid paid for the beneficiary's treatment from that third party. Recent court cases limited states' ability to recover from such judgments to the medical care costs, not the entire settlement, or the settlement amounts attributable to lost wages or non-medical costs.[12]

The Bipartisan Budget Act of 2013 (P.L. 113-67), Section 202, Strengthening Medicaid Third-Party Liability, amended the SSA to enable states to recover all portions of judgments received by Medicaid beneficiaries. In addition, Section 202 clarified that states may impose liens against Medicaid beneficiaries' property. These changes were effective October 1, 2014. PAMA Section 211 delayed the effective date of the beneficiary liability settlement amendment from October 1, 2014, until October 1, 2016.

This provision of H.R. 2 would extend the effective date of the beneficiary liability settlements from October 1, 2016, until October 1, 2017.

Section 221: Extension of Funding for Community Health Centers, the National Health Service Corps, and Teaching Health Centers

The ACA created the Community Health Center Fund (CHCF) that provided mandatory funding for federal health centers authorized in PHSA Section 330.[13] These centers are located in medically underserved areas and provide primary care, dental care, and other health and supportive services to individuals regardless of their ability to pay. Specifically, Section 10503 of the ACA (as amended by the Health Care and Education Reconciliation Act of 2010, P.L. 111- 152, §2303) appropriated a total of $9.5 billion from FY2011 through FY2015 annually as follows: $1.0 billion for FY2011; $1.2 billion for FY2012; $1.5 billion for FY2013; $2.2 billion for FY2014; and $3.6 billion for FY2015. Funds are to remain available until expended. The CHCF also provided funding for the National Health Service Corps (NHSC), authorized in Title III of the PHSA, which provides scholarships and loan repayments to certain health professionals in exchange for providing care in a health professional shortage area for a period of time that varies based on the length of the scholarship or the number of years of loan repayment received.[14] Specifically, the CHCF provided $1.5 billion for the NHSC from FY2011through FY2015 annually as follows: $290 million for FY2011; $295 million for FY2012; $300 million for FY2013; $305 million for FY2014; and $310 million for FY2015. Funds are to remain available until expended. ACA Section 5508 created PHSA Section 340H, which required the Secretary to make direct and indirect graduate medical education (GME) payments to qualified teaching health centers: community-based outpatient facilities that train medical residents. The section also appropriated $230 million in direct and indirect GME payments for the period of FY2011 through FY2015.

This provision would extend the CHCF by providing funding for health centers and the NHSC at the FY2015 level ($3.6 billion for health centers and $310 million for the NHSC) for each of FY2016 and FY2017 and would provide $60 million for each of FY2016 and FY2017 to support direct and indirect GME payments to teaching health centers. This section would also apply an existing restriction on the use of funds for abortions—included in P.L. 113-235, Division G, Title V, Sections 506-507,[15] which provided appropriations for FY2015—to funds that would be appropriated by this act to health centers, the NHSC, and qualified teaching health centers for FY2016 and FY2017.

Title III—CHIP

Section 301: Two-Year Extension of the Children's Health Insurance Program

Section 301(a): Funding

Federal funding for the State Children's Health Insurance Program (CHIP) is provided through FY2015 with appropriated amounts as specified in statute.[16] Since CHIP was established, other federal laws have provided additional years of federal CHIP funding. For instance, the Children's Health Insurance Program Reauthorization Act of 2009 (CHIPRA; P.L. 111-3) provided federal CHIP funding for FY2009 through FY2013. The ACA provided federal CHIP funding for an additional two years, with FY2015 being the last year of federal CHIP funding under current law.

For FY2014 and FY2015, the annual appropriation amounts are $19.1 billion and $21.1 billion, respectively. The FY2015 appropriation is the combination of semiannual appropriations of $2.85 billion from Section 2104(a) of SSA plus a one-time appropriation in the amount of $15.36 billion from Section 108 of CHIPRA, which is provided for the first six months of the fiscal year and remains available until expended.

Section 301(a) of H.R. 2 would extend federal CHIP funding for two years by adding federal appropriations for FY2016 and FY2017. The funding amounts are $19.30 billion for FY2016 and $20.40 billion for FY2017. The funding for FY2017 would be structured as it is for FY2015, with semiannual appropriations of $2.85 billion plus a one-time appropriation (discussed below) in the amount of $14.70 billion.

Section 301(b)(1) and (2): Allotments

The federal government reimburses states for a portion of every dollar they spend on CHIP up to state-specific annual limits called allotments, which are the federal funds allocated to each state for the federal share of its CHIP expenditures. State CHIP allotment funds are provided annually, and the funds are available to states for two years. There are two formulas for determining state allotments: an even-year formula and an odd-year formula.

In even years, such as FY2014, state CHIP allotments are based on each state's *allotment* for the prior year plus any Child Enrollment Contingency Fund payments (described below) from the previous year adjusted for growth in per capita National Health Expenditures and child population in the state. For even years, the allotment amount can be adjusted to reflect CHIP eligibility or benefit expansions.

In odd years, state CHIP allotments are each state's *spending* for the prior year (including federal CHIP payments from the state CHIP allotment, Child Enrollment Contingency Fund payments, and redistribution funds) adjusted using the same growth factor as the even-year formula (i.e., growth in per capita National Health Expenditures and child population in the state). Since the odd-year formula is based on states' actual use of CHIP funds, it is called the *rebasing year*, and a state's CHIP allotment can either increase or decrease depending on that state's CHIP expenditures in the previous year.

Under current law, FY2015 is the last year CHIP allotments are authorized. Section 301(b)(1) and (2) of H.R. 2 would authorize CHIP allotments for FY2016 and thereafter maintaining the allotment formulas for odd- and even-year allotments.

Section 301(b)(1)(B)(ii): Special Rule for FY2016

The federal government pays about 70% of CHIP expenditures, and the federal government's share of CHIP expenditures (including both services and administration) is determined by the enhanced federal medical assistance percentage (E-FMAP) rate. The E-FMAP rate is derived each year by the Secretary of HHS using a set formula, and it varies by state. By statute, the E-FMAP (or federal matching rate) can range from 65% to 85%, and in FY2015, the E-FMAP ranges from 65% (13 states) to 82% (Mississippi).

The ACA included a provision to increase the E-FMAP rate by 23 percentage points (not to exceed 100%) for most CHIP expenditures from

FY2016 through FY2019. This will increase the statutory range of the E-FMAP rate to 88% through 100%. With this 23 percentage point increase, the federal share of CHIP will be significantly higher, which means states are expected to spend through their allotments faster when the 23 percentage point E-FMAP increase takes effect.

Section 301(b)(1)(B)(ii) of H.R. 2 includes a special rule for the FY2016 allotments to account for the 23 percentage point increase in the E-FMAP that begins in FY2016. Under this provision, the FY2016 allotments would be each state's FY2015 *allotment* (including Child Enrollment Contingency Fund payments and redistribution funds) but determined as if the 23 percentage point increase in the E-FMAP were in place for FY2015. Then, that amount would be adjusted using the same growth factor as the even- and odd-year formulas (i.e., growth in per capita National Health Expenditures and child population in the state).

Section 301(b)(1)(B)(ii): Reduction in FY2018

State CHIP allotment funds are provided annually, and the funds are available to states for two years. After two years, any unused state CHIP allotment funds are redistributed to states with funding shortfalls. Although FY2017 is the last year for which federal CHIP funding is provided under H.R. 2, states could have federal CHIP spending in FY2018 because states will have access to unspent funds from their FY2017 allotments and to unspent FY2016 allotments redistributed to shortfall states. Section 301(b)(1)(B)(ii) of H.R. 2 includes a provision that would reduce the amount of states' unspent funds from their FY2017 allotments available for expenditures in FY2018 by one-third.

Section 301(b)(1)(C): Allotment for FY2017

Under current law, CHIP allotments for the first half of the FY2015 are available from the appropriation amount provided in Section 2104(a)(18)(A) of SSA in addition to the FY2015 onetime appropriation provided for in Section 108 of CHIPRA (discussed below). For the second half of the year, allotments are to be made available from the funding provided in the first half of the year in addition to the appropriation amount provided in Section 2104(a)(18)(B) of SSA.

In FY2015, the full-year amount for state allotments is to be equal to federal payments from the prior year (including Child Enrollment Contingency Fund payments and redistributed funds) multiplied by the allotment increase factor.

Section 301(b)(1)(C) of H.R. 2 includes a provision that would make the allotment formula for FY2017 the same as the formula for FY2015. For FY2017, funding for the first half of the year would be available from Section 2104(a)(20)(A) of SSA in addition to the FY2017 one-time appropriation provided for in Section 301(b)(3) of H.R. 2, and the funding for the second half of the year would be provided in Section 2104(a)(20)(B) of SSA.

Section 301(b)(3): One-Time Appropriation for FY2017

A one-time appropriation in the amount of $15.4 billion is provided for allotments for the first six months of FY2015 in addition to the semiannual appropriations provided in Section 2104(a)(18)(A) of SSA. The funds from the one-time appropriation are to remain available until expended.

CHIPRA provided a one-time appropriation for FY2013 (which was the last year of federal CHIP funding provided in CHIPRA) through Section 108 of CHIPRA. When the ACA added two years of federal CHIP financing, it provided the one-time appropriation for FY2015 (which was the last year of federal CHIP funding provided in ACA) by amending Section 108 of CHIPRA.

Section 301(b)(3) of H.R. 2 would provide a one-time appropriation in the amount of $14.7 billion for FY2017. This funding would accompany the allotments for the first half of FY2017, and the funding would remain available until expended. In addition, rather than amend Section 108 of CHIPRA as was done in the ACA for the FY2015 one-time appropriation, H.R. 2 includes the one-time appropriation language.

Section 301(c): Extension of Qualifying State Option

In a few situations, federal CHIP funding is used to finance Medicaid expenditures. For instance, certain states had significantly expanded Medicaid eligibility for children prior to the enactment of CHIP in 1997, and these states are allowed to use their CHIP allotment funds to finance the difference between the Medicaid and CHIP matching rates (i.e., FMAP and E-FMAP rates, respectively) for the cost of children in Medicaid in families with income above 133% FPL. The following 11 states meet the definition: Connecticut, Hawaii, Maryland, Minnesota, New Hampshire, New Mexico, Rhode Island, Tennessee, Vermont, Washington, and Wisconsin. This is referred to as the *qualifying state* option, and FY2015 is the last year in which the qualifying state option is authorized.

Section 301(c) of H.R. 2 would extend the qualifying state option through FY2017.

Section 301(d): Child Enrollment Contingency Fund

CHIPRA established the Child Enrollment Contingency Fund to provide shortfall funding to certain states. The Child Enrollment Contingency Fund was funded with an initial deposit equal to 20% of the appropriated amount for FY2009 (i.e., $2.1 billion). In addition, for FY2010 through FY2015, such sums as are necessary for making Child Enrollment Contingency Fund payments to eligible states are deposited into this fund, but these transfers cannot exceed 20% of the appropriated amount for the fiscal year or period.

For FY2009 through FY2015, states with a funding shortfall and CHIP enrollment for children exceeding a state-specific target level shall receive a payment from the Child Enrollment Contingency Fund equal to the amount by which the enrollment exceeds the target multiplied by the product of projected per capita expenditures and the E-FMAP.

Section 301(d) of H.R. 2 would extend the funding mechanism for the Child Enrollment Contingency Fund and payments from the fund through FY2017.

Section 302: Extension of "Express Lane" Eligibility

CHIPRA created a state plan option for "Express Lane" eligibility through September 30, 2013, whereby states are permitted to rely on a finding from specified "Express Lane" agencies (e.g., those that administer programs such as TANF, Medicaid, CHIP, and the Supplemental Nutrition Assistance Program, or SNAP) for (1) determinations of whether a child has met one or more of the eligibility requirements necessary to determine his or her initial eligibility, (2) eligibility redeterminations, or (3) renewal of eligibility coverage under Medicaid or CHIP. This provision was extended through subsequent legislation. Under current law, authority for "Express Lane" eligibility determinations expires after September 30, 2015.

H.R. 2 would extend authority for "Express Lane" eligibility determinations through September 30, 2017.

Section 303: Extension of Outreach and Enrollment Program

CHIPRA authorized $100 million in outreach and enrollment grants for fiscal years 2009 through 2013 to be used by eligible entities (e.g., states, local governments, community-based organizations, elementary or secondary schools) to conduct outreach and enrollment efforts that increase the participation of Medicaid and CHIP-eligible children. Ten percent of the allocation is directed to a national enrollment campaign to improve the enrollment of underserved child populations, and 10% is targeted to outreach for Native American children. The remaining 80% is distributed among eligible entities for the purpose of conducting outreach campaigns, focusing on rural areas and underserved populations. Grant funds also are targeted to proposals that address cultural and linguistic barriers to enrollment. The ACA appropriated $140 million for fiscal years 2009 through 2015 for outreach and enrollment grants. Authority for outreach and enrollment grants will expire after September 30, 2015.

H.R. 2 would authorize $40 million for fiscal years 2016 and 2017 for outreach and enrollment grants.

Section 304: Extension of Certain Programs and Demonstration Projects

Section 304(a): Childhood Obesity Demonstration Project

Section 401(a) of CHIPRA required the Secretary of HHS to conduct a childhood obesity demonstration project by awarding grants to eligible entities (e.g., community-based organizations, federally qualified health centers, universities, and colleges) to carry out individual programs. CHIPRA authorized the appropriation of $25 million for the period FY2009 through FY2013 for this demonstration, and ACA Section 4306 replaced the authorization of appropriation with a total appropriation of $25 million for the period of FY2010 through FY2014.

While Section 4306 of the ACA funds the demonstration project, CHIPRA provides guidance on program development and implementation. Grantees may use funds to develop, implement, and evaluate multilevel (e.g., child, family, community, policy), multisectoral (e.g., child care, school, community, health care) intervention projects, targeting communities with a high proportion of CHIP-eligible children. Authorized uses of funds include developing community educational activities that promote healthy eating behaviors; developing school-based after-hours physical activity programs; and training health professionals on how to identify and treat obese and overweight individuals.

Funding priority is granted to certain eligible entities such as those that can demonstrate having previously received funds to carry out activities that promote individual and community health; those that carry out programs or activities consistent with goals set by *Healthy People 2010*; or those located in medically underserved communities or areas in which the average poverty rate is at least 150% of the average poverty rate.

Under current law, funding for the childhood obesity demonstration project expired in FY2014, and funding was not appropriated for FY2015. In 2011, the Centers for Disease Control and Prevention awarded ACA funds to grantees for the period of FY2011 through FY2015.

The provision would extend funding for the childhood obesity demonstration project through FY2017, appropriating $10 million for the period of FY2016 through FY2017.

Section 304(b): Extension of Certain Programs and Demonstration Projects— Pediatric Quality Measures Program

Under current law, the Secretary was required to identify and publish an initial core set of pediatric quality measures by no later than January 1, 2010. The Secretary, not later than January 1, 2011, and every three years thereafter, also is required to submit a report to Congress on, for example, the quality of children's health care under Medicaid and CHIP. A Pediatric Quality Measures Program (PQMP) was required to be established by January 1, 2011; this program is required to identify pediatric measure gaps and development priorities, award grants and contracts to develop measures, and revise and strengthen the core measure set, among other things. States are required to submit reports to the Secretary annually to include, for example, information about state-specific child health quality measures applied by the state. The Secretary is required to collect, analyze, and make publicly available the information reported by states by not later than September 30, 2010, and annually thereafter. The Secretary was required, between FY2009 and FY2013, to award no more than 10 grants to states for demonstration projects to evaluate ideas to improve the quality of children's health care. In addition, the Secretary, not later than January 1, 2010, was required to establish a program to encourage the development and dissemination of a model electronic health record for children. The Institute of Medicine (IOM) was required to develop a report on the measurement of child health status and quality by no later than July 1, 2010.

Funding for these activities was appropriated in the amount of $45 million for each of FY2009 through FY2013. Section 210 of PAMA extended funding only for the PQMP for FY2014 by requiring that $15 million of the $60 million appropriated under Section 1139B(e) of SSA for FY2014 be used to carry out Section 1139A(b). The appropriation in Section 1139A(i) for funding to carry out Section 1139A (except for 1139A(e), the childhood obesity demonstration project) expired in FY2013; the funding designated to carry out Section 1139A(b) expired in FY2014.

This provision would appropriate $20 million for the period FY2016 and FY2017 for the purposes of carrying out Section 1139A. This funding would be specifically excluded from being used to carry out the activities under Section 1139A(e), the childhood obesity demonstration project; Section 1139A(f), the development of a model electronic health record for children; and Section 1139A(g), the IOM study of pediatric health quality.

Section 305: Report of Inspector General of HHS on Use of "Express Lane" Option Under Medicaid and CHIP

H.R. 2 would require the Inspector General of the Department of HHS to submit a report to the House Committee on Energy and Commerce and the Senate Committee on Finance not later than 18 months after the date of enactment of this act. The report would (1) include data on the number of individuals enrolled in Medicaid and CHIP through the Express Lane Eligibility (ELE) state plan option, (2) assess the extent to which individuals enrolled through ELE meet the eligibility requirements for Medicaid or CHIP, and (3) provide data on Medicaid and CHIP federal and state expenditures under ELE that is disaggregated between expenditures associated with individuals who meet the Medicaid or CHIP eligibility requirements, and those who do not.

Title IV—Offsets

Subtitle A. Medicare Beneficiary Reforms

Section 401: Limitation on Certain Medigap Policies for Newly Eligible Medicare Beneficiaries

Medicare Supplemental Health Insurance, more commonly referred to as "Medigap," is private health insurance that supplements Medicare coverage. It typically covers some or all of Medicare's deductibles and coinsurance, and it also may include additional items or services not covered by Medicare, such as coverage while traveling overseas. Medigap is available to Medicare beneficiaries who are enrolled in Medicare Parts A and B. Individuals who purchase Medigap must pay a monthly premium, which is set by and paid to the insurance company selling the policy. There are 10 standardized Medigap plans with varying levels of coverage. Two of the 10 standardized plans, Plans C and F, cover Medicare Parts A and B deductibles and coinsurance in full (i.e., offer *first-dollar* coverage). In 2013, about 66% of all Medigap enrollees were covered by one of these two plans. Two other plans, D and G are similar, respectively, to Plans C and F but do not cover Medicare Part B deductibles. (The 2015 Part B deductible is $147.)

Three states (Massachusetts, Minnesota, and Wisconsin) offer their own state-standardized Medigap Plans under waivers.

Beginning in 2020, this H.R. 2 provision would prohibit the sale of Medigap policies that cover Part B deductibles to newly eligible Medicare beneficiaries. This includes individuals who become eligible for Medicare due to age, disability or end-stage renal disease on or after January 1, 2020. This prohibition would also apply in waiver states. Entities who sell such policies after that time would be subject to fines, and/or imprisonment of not more than five years, and/or civil money penalties of not more than $25,000 for each prohibited act.[17] For newly eligible beneficiaries, references in the law to Medigap plans C and F would be deemed as references to plans D and G.

Section 402: Income-Related Premium Adjustment for Parts B and D

For the first 41 years of the Medicare program, all Part B enrollees paid the same Part B premium amounts regardless of their income. However, the MMA[18] required that, beginning in 2007, higher-income Part B enrollees pay higher premiums. Similarly, when the Part D program began in 2006, all enrollees in the same Part D plan paid the same premiums. The ACA subsequently imposed high-income premiums for Medicare Part D prescription drug benefit enrollees beginning in 2011. CMS estimates that fewer than 5% of Medicare beneficiaries pay these higher premiums.

For Medicare Part B, standard premiums (i.e., premiums paid by enrollees who are not considered high income) are set at 25% of average annual per capita Part B program expenditures.[19] Similarly, under Part D, base premiums are set at 25.5% of expected per capita costs for basic Part D coverage.[20] Adjustments are made to the Parts B and D premiums for higher-income beneficiaries, with the percentage of per capita expenditures paid by these beneficiaries increasing with income. This percentage ranges from 35% to 80% of average per capita expenditures for both Parts B and D. In 2015, individuals whose income exceeds $85,000 ($170,000 for a couple) are subject to higher premium amounts. (See Table 2, below.)

The ACA also required that the income thresholds used to determine Parts B and D high-income premiums for 2011 through 2019 be frozen at the 2010 levels.[21] Prior to 2010, annual adjustments to these levels were based on annual changes in the consumer price index for urban consumers (CPI-U), rounded to the nearest $1,000. However, the ACA froze the income thresholds and ranges at the 2010 level through 2019, rather than allowing them to rise with inflation. In other words, the income categories shown in Table 2 remain the same for years 2010 through 2019. This means that over time, as income, including Social Security benefits, increases with inflation, a greater proportion of Medicare enrollees must pay the high-income premiums. Beginning in 2020, the income thresholds are to revert to the levels they would have reached had they been indexed for inflation since 2007, thereby reducing the proportion of beneficiaries who are subject to higher premiums. Additionally, beginning in 2020, thresholds are to be adjusted annually again by changes in the CPI-U.

Table 2. Current Monthly Medicare Part B Premiums and Part D Premium Adjustments

Beneficiaries Who File Individual Tax Returns with Income (for couples, double the below figures):	Applicable Percentage	2015 Monthly Part B Premiums	2015 Monthly Part D Premium Adjustment
Less Than or Equal to $85,000	25%	$104.90	$0.0
Greater Than $85,000 and Less Than or			
Equal to $107,000	35%	$146.90	$12.30
Greater Than $107,000 and Less Than or			
Equal to $160,000	50%	$209.80	$31.80
Greater Than $160,000 and Less Than or			
Equal to $214,000	65%	$272.70	$51.30
Greater Than $214,000	80%	$335.70	$70.80

Source: CMS regulation for 2015 Part B premiums: http://www.gpo.gov/fdsys/pkg/FR-2014-10-10/pdf/2014- 24248.pdf and CMS Notice for 2015 Part D high-income adjustments: http://www.cms.gov/Medicare/HealthPlans/MedicareAdvtgSpecRateStats/Downloads/PartDandMABenchmarks2015.pdf.

Notes: The Part B column shows the full premium. The Part D column represents the high-income adjustment that is added onto the Part D drug plan premium, which can vary among plans.

Beginning in 2018, this provision of H.R. 2 would lower the income thresholds for the top two income groups as shown in Table 3, below. Individuals with incomes between $133,500 and $160,000 per year would be in the 65% applicable percentage group (instead of those with incomes between $160,000 and $214,000), and the income threshold for the highest group (80%) would be $160,000 (instead of $214,000).

Table 3. Proposed Income Thresholds for High-Income Premiums

Beneficiaries Who File Individual Tax Returns with Income:	Applicable Percentage
Less Than or Equal to $85,000	25%
More Than $85,000 but Not More Than $107,000	35%
More Than $107,000 but Not More Than $133,500	50%
More Than $133,500 but Not More Than $160,000	65%
More Than $160,000	80%

Source: Section 402 of the Medicare Access and CHIP Reauthorization Act of 2015 (H.R. 2).

Under this provision of H.R. 2, the income thresholds would stay at the current levels (in Table 2) through 2017 and would be at the new designated levels for 2018 and 2019 (shown in Table 3). For years 2020 and thereafter, the thresholds would be adjusted annually for inflation based on the CPI-U. However, unlike current law, the adjustments would be based on the new (2018) thresholds levels rather than being based on what the levels would have been without a freeze.

Subtitle B. Other Offsets

Section 411: Medicare Payment Updates for Post-acute Providers

Medicare payment amounts typically are updated each fiscal or calendar year to address potential yearly changes in the cost of health care items and services. The ACA reduced the annual update policy for post-acute care providers—skilled nursing facilities (SNFs), inpatient rehabilitation facilities (IRFs), long-term care hospitals (LTCHs), home health agencies (HHAs), and hospices—by including an adjustment to account for economy-wide productivity improvements that result in cost savings. The productivity adjustment for SNFs, IRFs, LTCHs, was implemented on October 1, 2011. The productivity adjustment for hospices was implemented on October 1, 2012, and January 1, 2015, for HHAs. The annual payment updates for SNFs, IRFs, LTCHs, HHAs and hospices may be subject to other statutory reductions (e.g., failure to report quality data) and administrative reductions (e.g., nominal case-mix growth) as well. Post-acute care providers and hospices may be subject to an update less than zero that would result in a lower payment rate than in the preceding year.

For FY2015, CMS administratively determined the annual Medicare payment update, after application of the productivity adjustment, to be 2.0% for SNFs, 2.2% for IRFs, 1.1% for LTCHs, and 2.1% for hospices. These payment rates may be subject to other administrative reductions as well. For CY2015, CMS administratively determined the annual Medicare payment update, after application of the productivity adjustment, to be 2.1% for HHAs; however, after application of the rebasing reduction required by the ACA, the net Medicare payment update for HHAs is 0%.

HHAs may be subject to other payment reductions as well. CMS has not yet proposed payment rate updates for these providers for rate-setting years 2016 and later.

H.R. 2 requires Medicare payment updates for SNFs, IRFs, LTCHs, and hospices to be 1% for FY2018 and 1% for HHAs for CY2018, after application of the productivity adjustment.

Section 412: Delay of Reduction to Medicaid Disproportionate Share Hospital Allotments

The Medicaid statute requires states to make disproportionate share hospital (DSH) payments to hospitals treating large numbers of low-income patients.[22] The federal government provides each state an annual DSH allotment, which is the maximum amount of federal matching funds that each state can claim for Medicaid DSH payments. The ACA included a provision directing the Secretary to make aggregate reductions in Medicaid DSH allotments in specified annual amounts for FY2014 through FY2020. Since the ACA, a number of laws have amended the ACA Medicaid DSH reductions by eliminating the reductions for FY2014 through FY2016, changing the reduction amounts, and extending the reductions through FY2024.

This provision would further amend the Medicaid DSH reductions by pushing the Medicaid DSH reductions out one year (i.e., eliminating the FY2017 reductions and extending the reductions to FY2025) and increasing the aggregate reduction amounts from $35.1 billion to $43.0 billion. Specifically, under this provision, the annual aggregate reductions to the Medicaid DSH allotments would equal to $2.0 billion in FY2018, $3.0 billion in FY2019, $4.0 billion in FY2020, $5.0 billion in FY2021, $6.0 billion in FY2022, $7.0 billion in FY2023, $8.0 billion in FY2024, and $8.0 billion in FY2025. In FY2026, states' DSH allotments would rebound to their prereduced levels with the annual inflation adjustments for FY2018 through FY2025.

Section 413: Levy on Delinquent Providers

Under the Federal Payment Levy Program, the Internal Revenue Service and the Department of the Treasury may collect overdue taxes through a continuous levy on certain federal payments, including Medicare FFS payments. The MIPPA required that CMS fully implement the requirements of the federal levy program. For outstanding tax debts, the federal levy program authorizes the government to reduce the payment owed to providers or suppliers by 15%, or by the exact amount of the tax owed if it is less than 15% of the payment. The maximum levy is increased to 100% for payments to government contractors and to 30% for payments due to Medicare providers and suppliers under SSA Title XVIII.

This provision of H.R. 2 would increase the percentage of Medicare provider and supplier payments subject to continuous federal levy from 30% to 100%. This provision would be applicable to payments made 180 days after enactment of this law.

Section 414: Adjustments to Inpatient Hospital Payment Rates

CMS modified its patient classification system and introduced Medicare severity-diagnosis related groups (MS-DRGs) into the Medicare IPPS starting for discharges in FY2008. In the FY2008 IPPS rule, CMS established prospective budget neutrality reductions of -1.2% in FY2008, -1.8% in FY2009, and -1.8% in FY2010 because of anticipated increases in measured severity of illness that would be attributable to documentation or coding improvements (DCI) associated with the new MS-DRGs.

The TMA, Abstinence Education, and QI Programs Extension Act of 2007 (P.L. 110-90) halved the CMS's planned DCI reductions in FY2008 and FY2009, but it permitted retrospective offsets to IPPS rate increases in FY2010, FY2011, and FY2012 to account for DCI payment increases in FY2008 and FY2009 above these amounts that were established through a retrospective claims evaluation. The law did not address the additional -1.8% decrease originally established by CMS for FY2010; CMS did not implement that DCI adjustment.

ATRA prevented CMS from fully recouping past overpayments related to DCI changes in FY2008 and FY2009. ATRA required CMS to establish additional base rate reductions that would recoup overpayments associated with DCI in FY2008, FY2009, and FY2010. CMS was directed to reduce the base rates in FY2014 through FY2017 to offset $11 billion in increased DCI payments from FY2008 through FY2013 that had not yet been recovered. This required adjustment did not affect the Secretary's authority to apply a prospective adjustment for DCI with respect to FY2010 discharges.

CMS implemented a schedule of a cumulative -0.8% reduction in each year from FY2014 to FY2017 (or an -0.8% reduction in FY2014; -1.6% reduction in FY2015; -2.4% reduction in FY2016; and -3.2% reduction in FY2017). In FY2018, CMS is expected to restore the cumulative -3.2% DCI reduction to the hospital base rate.

H.R. 2 would remove the authority to retroactively recoup DCI payment increases from FY2010. CMS would be directed to increase base rates +0.5 percentage points each year from FY2018 through FY2023 (for a total increase of +3.0 percentage points) instead of the anticipated increase of +3.2 percentage points in FY2018. CMS would be prohibited from recouping the additional 0.55 percentage point reduction in base rates to account for DCI payment increases in FY2010.

Title V—Miscellaneous

Subtitle A. Protecting the Integrity of Medicare

Section 501: Prohibition of Inclusion of Social Security Account Numbers on Medicare Cards

Beneficiaries' Social Security numbers (SSNs) are displayed on their Medicare cards. CMS uses the SSN to assign each beneficiary a health insurance claim number, which is required to document Medicare eligibility and most other administrative activities, including performance analysis and program integrity. With increasing identity theft, however, the display and use of the SSN on Medicare cards has raised the program's and beneficiaries' vulnerability to fraud. Thieves could steal the information from Medicare cards to commit identity theft, and beneficiaries are more vulnerable to data breaches—the unauthorized disclosure of a beneficiary's personally identifiable information.[23] CMS has proposed different options to remove SSNs from beneficiary identification cards, which have ranged in cost from $254 million to $316 million.[24]

H.R. 2 would require the Secretary to collaborate with the Commissioner of Social Security to establish cost-effective procedures to ensure that Medicare beneficiaries' SSNs (or a derivative) are not displayed, coded, or embedded on Medicare cards. To implement removal of beneficiary SSNs from Medicare cards, $320 million would be transferred from the Medicare Trust Funds to following accounts:

- the CMS Program Management Account—$65 million in FY2015 (available through FY2018); $53 million in FY2016 and $53 million in FY2017 (available through FY2018); and $48 million in FY2018 (available until expended).
- the Social Security Administration Limitation on Administration Account—$27 million in FY2015 (available until FY2018); $22 million in FY2016 and $22 million in FY2017 (available through FY2018); and $27 million in FY2018 (available until expended).
- the Railroad Retirement Board Limitation on Administration Account—$3 million in FY2015 (available until expended).

The Secretary would be required to set an effective date for removal of SSNs that was not later than four years after the date of enactment of H.R. 2.

Section 502: Preventing Wrongful Medicare Payments for Items and Services Furnished to Incarcerated Individuals, Individuals Not Lawfully Present, and Deceased Individuals

Medicare law and regulations generally prohibit payment for services for incarcerated beneficiaries.[25] However, there is an exception to this prohibition if state or local law requires incarcerated beneficiaries to repay the cost of medical services received while they are incarcerated and state or local governments enforce the requirement. Although there is a claim processing mechanism that allows CMS's contractors to identify provider claims that meet the exception requirements, data on incarcerated individuals is not always available before a claim is paid.[26] CMS's systems also are not always capable of identifying claims for incarcerated beneficiaries after they were paid so that overpayments could be recovered.

Medicare Part D sponsors submit claims information to CMS for each drug they dispense. CMS has processes that prevent Part D sponsors from paying claims that have dates of service more than 32 days after a beneficiary's death. The HHS Office of the Inspector General (OIG) found that CMS's policies allow Part D sponsors to pay for HIV drugs for deceased Medicare beneficiaries.[27]

Federal law prohibits unlawfully present aliens from receiving public benefits, including health benefits. CMS prohibited contractors from paying

Part A and B claims for unlawful aliens, but OIG found that some Part D claims were paid for unlawfully present individuals.[28] OIG noted that CMS and Part D plans did not have internal controls to identify and disenroll unlawful aliens and automatically reject Part D claims for those individuals.

H.R. 2 would amend the Social Security Act to require the Secretary to establish policies and claims edits that would prevent improper Medicare payments for incarcerated individuals, unlawfully present aliens, and deceased individuals. This provision also would require the OIG to submit a report to Congress on the procedures and maintenance of the process to ensure that Medicare did not make improper payments for incarcerated individuals, unlawfully present aliens, and deceased individuals. OIG would be required to submit an initial report within 18 months of the date of enactment of this law and periodically thereafter as determined necessary by the OIG.

Section 503: Consideration of Measures Regarding Medicare Beneficiary Smart Cards

Medicare beneficiaries' SSNs are displayed on their Medicare cards, exposing individuals to increased risk of identity theft and potential unauthorized disclosure of personal health information. A beneficiary's SSN is referred to as the health insurance claim number and is used for identification as well as for processing Medicare FFS claims and for other administrative activities.[29] Inclusion of individuals' SSNs on identification cards used to be a common practice, but in response to federal and state laws restricting using SSNs as identifiers, most organizations have abandoned that approach. CMS has proposed different options to remove SSNs from beneficiary identification cards which have ranged in cost from $254 million to $316 million.[30] In reviewing different methodologies to remove SSNs from Medicare cards, CMS officials have ruled out some options, such as embedding the number in smart cards or magnetic strips, because these options have been determined to be too costly, technically infeasible, or burdensome to providers and beneficiaries.[31]

H.R. 2 would enable the Secretary to assess whether it is cost-effective and technologically viable to use electronic Medicare cards. Electronic cards might include smart-card technology, such as an embedded and secure integrated circuit chip.[32] If the Secretary considers the feasibility of using smart-card technology, then the Secretary would be required to submit a report outlining the Secretary's consideration of electronic Medicare cards to the House Committees on Ways and Means and Energy and Commerce and to the Senate Committee on Finance.

Section 504: Modifying Medicare's Durable Medical Equipment Face-to-Face Encounter Documentation Requirement

Medicare covers certain durable medical equipment, prosthetics, orthotics, and supplies (DMEPOS) under Part B of the program if the DMEPOS are medically reasonable and necessary and prescribed by a physician. At least two places in the Medicare statutes either require that a face-to-face evaluation of a beneficiary be conducted as a condition for payment or give the Secretary authority to require such evaluations as a condition for payment. Specifically, the Secretary is statutorily prohibited from paying for a power wheelchair unless a physician, physician assistant, nurse practitioner, or clinical nurse specialist has conducted a face-to-face examination of the beneficiary and written a prescription. For power wheelchairs, each of the specified medical providers is able to perform and document the face-to-face examination. A separate provision of statute not pertaining to power wheelchairs gives the Secretary authority to require that payment be made for items and services only if a physician has communicated to the supplier a written order for the item prior to delivery of the item (WOPD). The ACA specified that only physicians were able to document a face-to-face encounter for such WOPD items, regardless of whether a physician, physician assistant, nurse practitioner, or clinical nurse specialist had conducted the face-to-face encounter.

H.R. 2 would authorize a physician, physician assistant, nurse practitioner, or clinical nurse specialist to document the face-to-face encounters that they themselves conduct. This would make the requirement similar to the face-to-face requirement for power wheelchairs under Medicare. H.R. 2 would allow the Secretary to implement this section through program instructions or otherwise.

Section 505: Reducing Improper Medicare Payments

CMS relies on a variety of contractors to help administer the Medicare program, including Medicare administrative contractors (MACs) for FFS (Parts A and B) Medicare. MACs process Medicare claims, and serve as the primary operational contact between the FFS program, and Medicare's approximate 1.5 million health care providers and suppliers. Within their geographic service areas, each MAC is required to educate providers and their staffs about the fundamentals of the program, policies and procedures, new initiatives, and other significant changes. MACs also identify potential improper payment issues through analyses of provider inquiries, claim submission errors, medical review data, Comprehensive Error Rate Testing (CERT) data, and the Recovery Audit Program data.

In addition to MACs, CMS also relies on other contractors that support program integrity activities, such as recovery audit contractors (RACs). Unlike other Medicare contractors, RACs are compensated on a contingency fee basis—their only payment is a percentage of the amount of each improper payment they identify, regardless of whether the claim was an overpayment or underpayment. RAC contingency fees vary depending on the contractor, the type of claim, and the Part of Medicare. Overpayments identified by RACs are recouped by MACs and the amount of recouped funds less contingency fees paid to RACs and expenses for administering the RAC program are returned to the Medicare Trust Funds. RACs must return contingency fees when overpayments are overturned on appeals filed by Medicare providers and suppliers. In its annual FFS RAC program report to Congress, CMS reported that Part A and B RACs returned over $3.0 billion to the Medicare Trust Funds for FY2013.[33]

To identify improper payments, RACs use three types of review: automated, semiautomated, and complex reviews. Automated reviews rely solely on computer system "edits" that review the claim's coded information. Semiautomated reviews also rely on system edits and data analysis to identify coding and other errors, but RACs also may review additional documentation offered by providers to substantiate the claim information. In complex reviews, licensed medical professionals manually review claim information and related documentation, including medical records copies requested from providers. RAC coders and clinicians look to verify that provided services and supplies were covered by Medicare and were reasonable and medically necessary.

In FFS Medicare, RACs focus primarily on post-payment claim review and identification of overpayments to be recouped by MACs, although they also indirectly provide insight to CMS and other Medicare contractors on topics for provider education and outreach and identification of fraud and abuse vulnerabilities.

RAC overpayment decisions that are appealed by providers affect the amount identified by RACs and the amount returned to the Medicare Trust Funds. The Medicare FFS appeals process has four levels. If providers appeal a large number of corrected RAC claims and these claims are eventually overturned in providers' favor, then RAC corrections initially reported in annual reports overstate the success of the program. In addition, these appeals increase CMS's cost of administering the RAC program, since CMS must compensate MACs for their work in resolving appeals. Furthermore, appeals are costly for providers, although those costs are not borne by Medicare. The Medicare appeals process can take two years or more to resolve appealed claims (counting all appeal levels) and even longer if providers are unsuccessful and pursue their cases in District Court.

H.R. 2 would amend the SSA by adding a new requirement for MACs to implement an improper payment outreach and education program. Each MAC would be required to have such a program to provide outreach, education, training, and technical assistance activities to providers and suppliers in their geographic service areas. MACs would be required to provide these services on a regular basis. The information that would be provided by MACs under the improper payment outreach and education program would include information the Secretary determined to be appropriate, which may include the following:

- a list of each provider's and supplier's most frequent and expensive payment errors over the last quarter;
- specific instructions on how to correct or avoid these errors in the future;
- notice of all new audit topics that the Secretary has approved for RACs;
- specific instructions to prevent future issues related to new RAC procedures approved by the Secretary; and
- other information the Secretary determined would be appropriate.

MACs would be required under the outreach and education program to give priority to activities that would reduce Medicare improper payments that are one of the following:

- for items or services that have the highest rate of improper payment;
- for items and services that have the greatest total dollar amount of improper payments;
- due to clear misapplication or misinterpretation of Medicare policies;
- clearly due to common and inadvertent clerical or administrative errors; or
- due to other error types the Secretary determined could be prevented through activities under the outreach and education program.

To assist MACs in conducting the improper payment outreach and education program, the Secretary would be required to supply to each MAC a complete list of the types of improper payments identified by RACs for the providers and suppliers in the MACs region. The list of services identified by RACs and provided to each MAC would be supplied on a time frame determined appropriate by the Secretary, which may be quarterly. The list of improper payments identified by RACs that the Secretary would be required to supply to each MAC would include information such as the following:

- providers and suppliers that have the highest improper payment rates;
- providers and suppliers that have the greatest total dollar amounts of improper payments;
- items and services furnished in each MAC's service region that have the highest improper payment rates;
- items and services furnished in each MAC's service region that are responsible for the greatest total improper payment amounts; and
- other information the Secretary determines would be helpful to MACs in carrying out the outreach and education program.

MACs would be required to ensure that all provider and supplier communications related to the improper payment outreach and education programs complied with communication requirements identified in SSA Section 1874A(g), Communications with Beneficiaries, Providers, and Suppliers.

The SSA also would be amended at Section 1893(h) to authorize the Secretary to retain a portion of annual RAC overpayment recoveries, which would be available, subject to certain limitations (see below), to the CMS program management account for carrying out the activities of the following sections:

- SSA Section 1833(z), Incentive Payments for Participation in Eligible Alternative Payment Models;
- SSA Section 1834(1)(16), Prior Authorization for Repetitive Scheduled Non-Emergent Ambulance Transports;
- SSA Section 1874A(a)(4)(G), Additional Functions;[34]
- Medicare Access and CHIP Reauthorization Act of 2015, Section 514(b); and
- implementing strategies (such as claim processing edits) to help reduce Medicare payment error rates.

The amounts retained from RAC overpayment recoveries would be limited to 15% of RAC recoveries and would remain available until expended. The Secretary would be prohibited from using the funds retained from RAC overpayment recoveries for technology-related infrastructure, capital investments, or information systems, except for uses that supported claims processing (including edits) or system functionality for detecting fraud. In addition, in retaining an additional portion of RAC overpayment recoveries, contingency fee payments to RACs would not be reduced.

Section 506: Improving Senior Medicare Patrol and Fraud Reporting Rewards

Section 203(b) of the Health Insurance Portability and Accountability Act of 1996 (HIPAA; P.L. 109-141) established an Incentive Reward Program to collect information on Medicare fraud and abuse. The program encourages individuals to report to the HHS Secretary information on those who engage in certain violations under the SSA, including those who engage in fraud and abuse against the Medicare program. If an individual reports information that serves as the basis for collection they may be paid a portion of the amount collected.

Section 411 of the Older Americans Act (OAA; P.L. 89-73, as amended) authorizes the Senior Medicare Patrol program, which funds projects that educate older Americans and their families to recognize and report Medicare fraud. The program engages volunteers to conduct outreach and education to Medicare beneficiaries about suspected fraud, errors, or abuse. The program also receives beneficiary complaints regarding suspected fraud or abuse and makes determinations about such complaints, which may result in referrals to the appropriate state and federal agencies for further investigation.

H.R. 2 would require the HHS Secretary to develop a plan to revise the Incentive Reward Program to encourage greater individual participation in the reporting of Medicare fraud and abuse. Such a plan would include recommendations for ways to enhance rewards for individuals reporting under the program and ways to extend the program to Medicaid. The plan would also include recommendations for the use of Senior Medicare Patrols to conduct a public awareness and education campaign to encourage participation in the revised incentive program. It would require the HHS Secretary to submit the plan to Congress no later than 180 days after enactment.

Section 507: Requiring Valid Prescriber National Provider Identifiers on Pharmacy Claims

To administer the Medicare Part D outpatient prescription drug benefit, CMS contracts with private companies, called plan sponsors, that provide benefits through drug plans. Medicare Part D drug plans provide Part D benefits to enrollees by contracting with pharmacies that fill prescriptions and submit claims and other data to CMS. CMS uses these data to monitor and administer the Part D benefit. Part D drug plans submit prescription drug data to CMS in an electronic, prescription drug event (PDE), record. The PDE contains drug cost and payment as well as other data, including the identification number of the provider who wrote the prescription, the enrollee, the pharmacy that filled the prescription, and drug information. CMS uses or requires Part D plans to use some of the PDE data, such as pharmacy and prescriber identifiers, to validate claims, monitor quality, and conduct program integrity and other oversight activities. There are several possible numbers that can be used to uniquely identify prescribers, including the national provider identifier (NPI), the Drug Enforcement Administration registration number, state license numbers, and the unique provider identification number. CMS is transitioning to using the NPI to identify all participating Medicare providers. CMS recommended that Part D plan sponsors prepare and review reports of physician drug prescribing patterns to identify potential prescriber fraud.[35] CMS, however, does not have system edits to check the prescriber identification data included in PDEs.[36] CMS does not require the prescriber identifier and other qualifying fields to be completed on certain non-standard format Part D claims, such as claims filed by beneficiaries and paper claims. In a June 2010 report, OIG found that there were a number of Part D claims with invalid prescriber identifiers and these claims accounted for $1.2 billion in Medicare Part D expenditures. OIG also reported that CMS and Part D plans did not have adequate procedures to detect invalid prescriber identifiers.

Beginning with Medicare Part D plan year (calendar year) 2016, H.R. 2 would require the Secretary to ensure that PDEs included the NPI to identify the prescribing provider and that the NPI is checked to determine that it is a valid number. In addition, the Secretary would also establish procedures to ensure that when a Part D claim is denied because of the NPI requirements, beneficiaries would be informed of the denial reason at the point of service. Moreover, OIG would be required to prepare a report to Congress by January 1, 2018, on the effectiveness of the procedures to require valid NPIs on all Part D drug claims.

Section 508: Option to Receive Medicare Summary Notice Electronically

The Medicare contractor that processes claims mails a Medicare Summary Notice (MSN) that identifies the health care services each beneficiary received during the previous quarter. MSNs are not bills, but they contain information about provider charges, the amount Medicare paid, and the amount for which beneficiaries were responsible. Medicare beneficiaries enrolled in FFS Medicare may view e-MSNs online and can print their MSNs from their own computer.[37]

H.R. 2 would require the Secretary, beginning January 1, 2017, to establish a process whereby beneficiaries may opt to receive MSNs electronically. If beneficiaries opt to receive their MSNs electronically, they would not also receive mailed MSNs. The provision gives the Secretary discretion to limit the number of elections beneficiaries may exercise, but not for the Secretary to limit the number of elections to less than one. The Secretary would be required to ensure in the most cost-effective manner that beginning January 1, 2017, beneficiaries received clear notification of the option to receive e-MSN statements, which may be distributed with mailed MSNs. Moreover, the Secretary would be required to apply an option similar to electronic MSN notices to other HHS areas and to provide MSNs or other notices on a more frequent basis than otherwise required.

Section 509: Renewal of Medicare Administrative Contractor Contracts

CMS administers the Medicare program through contracts with private entities, such as Medicare administrative contractors (MACs). MACs help CMS run Medicare's day-to-day operations by paying FFS claims, enrolling providers, handling provider customer service, providing education and outreach, administering appeals, operating toll-free call centers, and other activities. In addition, MACs conduct some program integrity activities, including prepayment and post-payment claims review, audits of hospitals and other institutional providers, and recoupment of overpayments. MACs also implement local coverage determinations (LCD) in their jurisdictions.

The MMA required the Secretary to implement Medicare FFS contracting reform by 2011. Contracting reform was designed to improve Medicare's administrative services to beneficiaries and health care providers through the use of new contracting tools including competition and performance incentives. CMS initiated a first round of Parts A and B FFS contractor reform by awarding contracts to 15 Parts A and B MACs (A/B MACs) and four DME

MACs between 2005 and 2010.[38] In 2010, CMS announced that it intended to further consolidate the 15 combined Parts A/B MAC contracts to 10 contract areas during a second round of MAC contract awards.[39] By February 2014, CMS had reduced the number of A/B MAC contract areas to 12 by combining contract areas when the contracts were re-competed. CMS also announced that it would postpone further Part A/B MAC contract area consolidation for up to five years.[40]

MAC performance is an important CMS management activity given the breadth of activities these contractors play in administering Medicare Parts A and B and the size of the contracts awarded to MACs. In a retrospective study OIG found that over a five year contracting period, CMS awarded $4.3 billion in contracts to 16 MACs.[41] Several CMS divisions within the Medicare Contractor Management Group have some responsibility in assessing performance, conducting oversight, and monitoring MAC activities. Under Medicare law MAC contracts are awarded for a base year with four option years.[42] CMS has discretion whether or not to exercise the option to renew MAC contracts for the option years.[43] In a 2013 report, OIG noted that the time period for re-competing MAC contracts might be better managed if it was longer. CMS could delay re-competing MAC contracts with successful contractors, while using the time saved from the successful contract re-compete contract cycles to spend more time replacing under-performing MACs.[44]

H.R. 2 would amend the SSA to extend the time period under which MAC contracts must be offered with the application of competitive procedures running for 10 years rather than the current 5-year period. This change would be applicable to new MAC contracts as well as contracts in effect as of the date of enactment of H.R. 2. In addition, the Secretary would be required, to the extent possible without compromising the MAC contracting process, to make available to the public the performance of each MAC with respect to performance requirements and measurement standards.

Section 510: Study on Pathway for Incentives to States for State Participation in Medicaid Data Match Program

CMS initiated the Medicare-Medicaid Data Match Program as a pilot program in 2001.[45] MediMedi was intended to help CMS and states identify overpayments and fraud that affected both Medicare and Medicaid. Based on comparative Medicare and Medicaid data, CMS investigated atypical billing patterns that may not have been evident when analyzing the data from each program separately. If problems were identified, CMS, through a contractor, coordinated with states (for Medicaid) and providers (for Medicare) to recover federal overpayments.

The Medi-Medi pilot was funded mostly by CMS with some addition support from the Federal Bureau of Investigation. California was the only state in the original pilot in 2001. In 2005, CMS was allocated $19 million from Health Care Fraud and Abuse Control (HCFAC) funds to continue the California Medi-Medi pilot and expand it to eight other states.[46] In 2006, Section 6034 of the Deficit Reduction Act of 2005 (DRA; P.L. 109-171) required the Secretary to expand the MediMedi program nationwide and established dedicated funding ($12 million in FY2006, rising to $60 million annually in FY2010 and every year thereafter).

In a 2012 report, OIG found that the Medi-Medi program had produced limited results and few fraud referrals.[47] During 2007 and 2008, CMS had Medi-Medi projects in 10 states, which produced about 66 fraud referrals to law enforcement, and 27 cases were accepted.[48] OIG also found that state Medicaid programs received less benefit from the Medi-Medi program than Medicare received.

H.R. 2 would require the Secretary to study and, as appropriate, specify incentives for states to work with the Secretary in conducting the Medi-Medi Data Match program. The Secretary would be authorized to use the limited waiver authority available in the Medi-Medi Data Match program to specify those state incentives.[49]

Section 511: Guidance on Application of Common Rule to Clinical Data Registries

The Physician Quality Reporting System (PQRS) was established by CMS to reward eligible professionals for reporting specified quality data to the agency. Section 601(b) of the American Taxpayer Relief Act of 2012 (SSA §1848(m)(3)(E)) required the Secretary of HHS to deem those eligible professionals who satisfactorily participate in a "qualified clinical data registry" as having met the quality reporting requirements for PQRS for 2014 and subsequent years. The section also required the Secretary to establish requirements for a qualified clinical data registry and in so doing to consider, among other things, whether an entity has mechanisms in place to ensure transparency and to support quality improvement initiatives for participants. Measures used in the qualified clinical data registries may be endorsed by the National Quality Forum (NQF). These measures are not subject to the process for measure selection being carried out by multi-stakeholder groups under Section 1890A of the SSA. In defining the requirements for the qualified clinical data registries, the Secretary was required to consult with interested parties and establish a process to determine whether the requirements have been met. GAO was required to conduct a study on the potential of clinical data registries to improve the quality and efficiency of care in the Medicare program, including through payment incentives. As required by statute, GAO submitted a report to Congress on this study in December 2013.[50]

Subpart A of Title 45, Part 46, of the *Code of Federal Regulations* (the Common Rule) outlines the basic HHS policy for the protection of human research subjects carried out using federal funding, as specified, including requirements for Institutional Review Board composition and review and informed consent, among other things.

This provision of H.R. 2 would require the Secretary, not later than one year after enactment, to issue a clarification or modification with respect to the application of the Common Rule (specifically, Subpart A of 45 C.F.R. 46) for the protection of human research subjects to activities involving clinical data registries, including qualified clinical data registries.

Section 512: Eliminating Certain Civil Money Penalties; Gainsharing Study and Report

Under Section 1128A of the SSA, the OIG is authorized to impose civil penalties and assessments on individuals and entities that engage in improper conduct with respect to federal health programs, including the imposition of penalties for knowingly presenting or causing to be presented to a federal or state employee or agent certain false or fraudulent claims.[51] These penalties also might be applicable to certain payments made to physicians to reduce or limit services. The Section 1128A penalties include fines up to $10,000 for each item or service found to be fraudulently claimed, and up to $50,000 under certain additional circumstances, as well as treble damages.

H.R. 2 would amend Section 1128A of the SSA to enable hospitals and critical access hospitals to compensate physicians for reducing medically unnecessary services provided to beneficiaries of federal health programs without being subject to civil monetary penalties. This provision would be effective on the date of enactment of H.R. 2.

In addition, the Secretary, in consultation with the OIG, would be required within 12 months after the enactment of H.R. 2 to study and submit a report to Congress that identifies options for amending existing SSA Titles XI and XVIII that provide exceptions, safe harbors, or other narrowly targeted fraud and abuse provisions. The intent of the study and report would be to identify gainsharing arrangements or other similar arrangements between physicians and hospitals that otherwise would be subject to civil monetary penalties and to improve care while reducing waste and increasing efficiency. The report to Congress would be required to include the following:

- consideration of whether gainsharing provisions should apply to ownership interests, compensation arrangements, and other relationships;
- description of how the recommendations address accountability, transparency, and quality, including how best to limit inducements to stint on care, discharge patients prematurely, or otherwise reduce or limit medically necessary care; and
- consideration of whether a portion of any savings generated by gainsharing and other arrangements (as compared to an historic benchmark or other metric specified by the Secretary to determine the effect of delivery and payment system changes on Medicare expenditures) should accrue to the Medicare program.

Section 513: Modification of Medicare Home Health Surety Bond Condition of Participation Requirement

Medicare covers part-time or intermittent home health services under both Parts A and B.[52] Home health services include skilled nursing services, physical and occupational therapy, speech therapy, medical social services, and home health aide services. Home health service providers consistently have been associated with high improper payment rates and other vulnerabilities.[53] CMS sometimes has been unable to collect home health agency improper payments. BBA97 required the Secretary to impose surety bonds on Medicare home health agencies. Regulations promulgated in 1998 set the surety bond amount at the greater of $50,000 or 15% of the annual amount paid in Medicare claims. Those regulations are pending. Congressional oversight agencies such as OIG and GAO recommended that CMS require surety bonds that would help to improve overpayment recoveries from home health agencies.

H.R. 2 would authorize the Secretary to require Medicare home health agencies to post a surety bond in a form specified by the Secretary of at least $50,000 or an amount commensurate with the volume of payments to the home health agency.

Section 514: Oversight of Medicare Coverage of Manual Manipulation of the Spine to Correct Subluxation

Medicare covers medically necessary chiropractic services, which are limited to certain manual (use of hands) spinal manipulation treatments to correct subluxations.[54] When submitting payment claims, chiropractors must indicate that their services were for acute/corrective treatment by attaching a modifier to their claims.[55] According to CMS guidance, chiropractors also must be able to provide certain specific documents to support claims for their services. When further improvement cannot reasonably be expected from continuing care, the services are considered maintenance therapy, which is not medically necessary and therefore not payable under Medicare.

In a 2009 study, GAO found that CMS's efforts to stop payments not covered by Medicare for chiropractic maintenance therapy were unsuccessful.[56] CMS, supported by MACs and program integrity contractors, has used a variety of initiatives including provider education, system edits (caps), and focused medical review, but it continues to identify a high number of improper payments for chiropractic services that are maintenance treatments.

H.R. 2 would require the Secretary to establish a medical review process applicable to certain chiropractic manipulation treatments to correct spinal subluxation provided to Medicare beneficiaries.[57] This medical review process would be applicable to the following types of chiropractic claims submitted after December 31, 2016:

- services provided by a chiropractor who had aberrant billing patterns in comparison to peers; and
- services by a chiropractor who in a prior period had a claim denial percentage in the 85th percentile or greater after adjusting for claims denials that were overturned on appeal.

The medical review that would be required by this provision would consist of prior authorization of claims furnished by an individual chiropractor that were part of an episode of treatment that included more than 12 services, based on a justification for treatment such as a diagnosis code.

The Secretary would be authorized to end the prior authorization medical review if the Secretary determines the chiropractor has a low denial rate under prior authorization, but the Secretary may reapply prior authorization medical review if it is determined to be appropriate since the time the prior authorization was lifted. Chiropractors would be permitted to request prior authorization medical review for their services before the chiropractor furnishes the 12th treatment during an episode of care.

The Secretary also would be authorized to use pre-payment or post-payment review of chiropractic services that were not subject to prior authorization medical review. The Secretary has discretion not to use prior authorization medical review in cases where fraud may be suspected. When chiropractor claims were subject to prior authorization medical review, the Secretary would be authorized to make a determination as to whether the services would meet the medical necessity requirements prior to the service being furnished.[58] The Secretary is prohibited from paying chiropractor claims subject to the prior authorization medical review unless the claims were determined to meet the medical necessity requirements. Chiropractors subject to the prior authorization medical review would be authorized to submit information to support the services they propose to provide by fax, mail, or electronic means. The Secretary would be required to facilitate the receipt of electronic documentation as soon as practicable. For chiropractor claims subject to the prior authorization medical review, the Secretary would be required to make a determination as to the medical necessity of services within 14 days of receipt of the medical documentation or the services could be provided without prior authorization.

When payment for chiropractic services was denied as a result of pre-payment or post-payment review—applied to claims not subject to prior authorization medical review—beneficiaries payment liability would be limited as stipulated in Section 1879 of the SSA.

The Secretary would be authorized to contract with MACs or any other Medicare contractors other than recovery audit contractors (RACs).

The Secretary would be required under this provision to apply the prior authorization medical review in a manner that would allow chiropractors to obtain authorization to provide multiple services at a single time rather than on a service-by-service basis.

Chiropractic services subject to prior authorization medical review also could be denied for failing to meet other applicable requirements.

The Secretary is authorized to implement the requirements for prior authorization medical review under this section by publishing an interim final rule with comment period. This provision would be exempt from the Federal Information Policy requirements under Chapter 35 of Title 44 of the *United States Code*.

The Secretary would be required to consult with stakeholders, including the American Chiropractic Association and MAC representatives, to develop educational and training programs to improve the ability of chiropractors to provide documentation that would demonstrate that these services are reasonable and necessary. The Secretary would be required to make the educational and training programs available by January 1, 2016.

The Secretary would be authorized to use funds recovered by RACs and authorized for use by Section 506(b) of H.R. 2 to implement this provision.

GAO would be required to conduct a study on the effectiveness of prior authorization medical review process of services furnished as manual manipulation treatments for subluxation of the spine. The GAO study would be required to include an analysis of the aggregate data on (1) the number of individuals, chiropractors, and claims for services subject to prior authorization medical review; (2) the number of prior authorization medical reviews conducted. In addition, the GAO report would be required to include an analysis of the outcome of the prior authorization medical review conducted.

Within four years after the date of enactment, GAO would be required to submit a report to Congress containing the results of its study on the prior authorization medical review of chiropractic services. The report would include recommendations for legislation and administrative action applicable to the process for prior authorization of chiropractic medical review as determined appropriate by GAO.

Section 515: National Expansion of Prior Authorization Model for Repetitive Scheduled Non-emergent Ambulance Transport

Medicare covers ambulance services, including non-emergent transportation, when furnished to a beneficiary whose medical condition is such that other means of transportation are contraindicated. CMS has defined a repetitive ambulance service as medically necessary ambulance transportation that is furnished in three round trips or more during a 10-day period, or at least once per week for at least three weeks.

Section 1115A of the SSA establishes the Center for Medicare and Medicaid Innovation and authorizes the testing of innovative payment and service delivery models to reduce expenditures while preserving or enhancing the quality of care furnished to Medicare, Medicaid, and CHIP beneficiaries. After evaluation, the scope and duration of the innovated payment and service delivery models that meet certain criteria can be expanded through rulemaking. Budget neutrality is not required as a condition for testing a new payment or service delivery model. However, the design or implementation of a model will be modified or terminated, unless the CMS Office of the Actuary certifies after testing has begun, that that model is expected (1) to improve quality of care without increasing spending, (2) reduce spending without reducing the quality of care, or, (3) improve the quality of care and reduce spending. There has been $15 billion in funding appropriated from FY2010 through FY2019 to implement new payment models.

CMS recently implemented a three-year prior authorization model for repetitive scheduled non-emergent ambulance transport in New Jersey, Pennsylvania, and South Carolina under the statutory authority at 1115A of the SSA. Ambulance suppliers (or beneficiaries) began submitting prior authorization requests on December 1, 2014, for transports occurring on or after December 15, 2014.

H.R. 2 would extend the prior authorization payment model for repetitive non-emergent transports to transports in Delaware, the District of Columbia, Maryland, New Jersey, Pennsylvania, North Carolina, South Carolina, West Virginia, and Virginia starting no later than January 1, 2016. The funding in 1115A of the SSA would be allocated to carry out this expansion.

The prior authorization model would be expanded to all states if deemed appropriate by the Secretary. The RAC recovery funds established in 1893(h)(10) of the SSA elsewhere in the legislation would be used to carry out this provision. The expansions of the prior authorization model would be required to meet the budget neutrality requirements under Section 1115A.

Section 516: Repealing Duplicative Medicare Secondary Payer Provision

Under Medicare Secondary Payer (MSP) laws, Medicare pays the medical bills of beneficiaries covered by certain group health plans and other types of insurance such as liability insurance, only after the other insurer has made the first, or primary, payment.[59] A provision of MSP law, Section 1862(b)(5) of the SSA (42 U.S.C. Section 1395y(b)(5)), requires employers to provide certain information regarding employees or spouses of employees who may be Medicare eligible and may have received group health benefits. The statute includes fines for employers that willfully and repeatedly decline to report the information of up to $1,000 for each individual for which a request for information has been made.

Subsequent legislation, Section 111 of the Medicare, Medicaid, and SCHIP Extension Act of 2007 (MMSEA; P.L. 110-173), included additional requirements for group health plans to provide information to HHS regarding the health insurance status of employees, as well as judgments, payments, or settlements involving Medicare beneficiaries. The information is used prospectively to determine whether Medicare is a primary or a secondary payer and retrospectively to collect reimbursement for erroneous payments and conditional payments.

This provision would eliminate the original reporting requirements under Section 1862(b)(5) for information required to be provided on or after July 1, 2016, to avoid duplication of reporting requirements. The amendment would take effect on the date of enactment and would apply to information required on or after January 1, 2016.

Section 517: Plan for Expanding Data in Annual Comprehensive Error Rate Testing Report

CMS implemented the Comprehensive Error Rate Testing (CERT) program to measure improper payments in the Medicare FFS program. CERT was designed to comply with the Improper Payments Information Act (IPIA; P.L. 107-300), as amended by the Improper Payments Elimination and Recovery Improvement Act of 2012 (IPERIA; P.L. 112-248). A CERT contractor selects a stratified random sample of approximately 40,000 Medicare Part A and B claims submitted and processed by MACs during each reporting period. The sample size was selected to enable CMS to calculate a national improper payment rate and contractor- and service-specific improper payment rates. After selecting the sampled claims, CMS's CERT contractor collects supporting documentation for each claim. The sampled claims and the supporting documentation are reviewed by an independent medical review contractor to determine if they were properly paid under Medicare coverage, coding, and billing rules. If these criteria are not met or the provider fails to submit medical records to support the claim, the claim is counted as either a total or partial improper payment and the improper payment may be recouped (for overpayments) or reimbursed (for underpayments). CMS then calculates an annual Medicare FFS improper payment rate. The Medicare FFS improper payment rate in FY2014 was 12.7% and the rate in FY2013 was 10.1%.[60]

H.R. 2 would require the Secretary to submit a report to the Senate Committee on Finance and the House of Representatives Committees on Energy and Commerce and Ways and Means by June 30, 2015, that includes the following information:

- a plan for including in the annual CERT program, data on services (or service groupings; other than medical visits) paid under the Medicare FFS physician fee schedule where the fee schedule amount was

greater than $250 and where the CERT rate for those services or service groupings also exceeded 20%; and
- to the extent practicable by June 30, 2015, specific examples of services or service groupings that had physician fee schedule payment amounts over $250 and had CERT rates greater than 20%.

Section 518: Removing Funds for Medicare Improvement Fund Added by IMPACT Act of 2014

A provision in the Improving Medicare Post-Acute Care Transformation Act of 2014 (IMPACT; P.L. 113-185) amended SSA Section 1898 to, among other changes, convert the Transitional Fund for Sustainable Growth Rate Reform to the Medicare Improvement Fund. IMPACT also appropriated $195 million to the fund to be available during and after FY2020.

H.R. 2 would amend Section 1898(b)(1) of the SSA to eliminate the $195 million appropriated for the Medicare Improvement Fund to be available during and after FY2020.

Section 519: Rule of Construction

Except as explicitly noted in H.R. 2, Subtitle A—Protecting the Integrity of Medicare—including amendments made by Subtitle A, H.R. 2 would not prevent the use of notice and comment rulemaking in the implementation of Subtitle A's provisions and amendments.

Subtitle B. Other Provisions

Section 521: Extension of Two-Midnight PAMA Rules on Certain Medical Review Activities

In August 2013, CMS established a policy regarding the determination of a medically necessary short inpatient stay. Under that policy, inpatient admissions are presumed to be medically appropriate if a physician expects a beneficiary's treatment to require a two-night hospital stay and admits the patient under that assumption. With this two-midnight rule, CMS thought that hospitals would have fewer incentives to provide outpatient observation services to beneficiaries.

These outpatient stays have higher out-of-pocket expenses for beneficiaries and do not count toward the three-day inpatient requirement for Medicare skilled nursing facility (SNF) coverage. CMS delayed enforcement of certain aspects of this policy until September 30, 2014. Specifically, Medicare's recovery audit contractors (RACs) did not conduct patient status reviews assessing the medical necessity of short inpatient stays with dates of service between October 1, 2013, and September 30, 2014. The Medicare administrative contractors (MACs) will monitor hospitals' compliance with the new regulations under a probe-and-educate program. These reviews are intended to be instructional and are limited to a sample of 10 claims to 25 claims per hospital. PAMA permits the MACs to conduct the probe-and-educate program for claims from October 1, 2014, through March 31, 2015. PAMA would not permit post-payment RAC audits for claims with dates of admission from October 1, 2013, through March 31, 2015, unless there is evidence of systematic gaming, fraud, abuse, or delays in the provision of care.

H.R. 2 would extend the MAC's probe-and-educate program for claims through FY2015. Post-payment RAC audits would not be permitted with dates of admission through September 30, 2015.

Section 522: Requiring Bid Surety Bonds and State Licensure for Entities Submitting Bids under the Medicare DMEPOS Competitive Acquisition Program

Medicare generally pays for most durable medical equipment, prosthetics, orthotics, and supplies (DMEPOS) on the basis of fee schedules. Fee schedules are statutorily determined formulas used to set payment amounts for equipment. Over time, the Medicare fee schedules for DMEPOS have resulted in payment amounts that are higher than amounts paid by other payers. The MMA required the Secretary to establish a competitive acquisition program (competitive bidding) to replace the Medicare fee schedules in the selected areas where competitive bidding takes place. Under competitive bidding, payments for specified pieces of equipment in specified areas are determined by the bids of winning suppliers. A bid represent the price at which a supplier is willing to provide equipment to Medicare beneficiaries. Suppliers bid on all of the items within a category of DMEPOS, such as hospital beds and supplies, or oxygen equipment and supplies. A supplier's bid for each item in a category is then weighted by national usage of the item and added together to create the supplier's "composite bid" for the category.

Suppliers compete based on price (i.e., their composite bid) only after meeting other specified competition criteria including the following: a supplier must meet financial standards; the supplier must meet quality requirements; each supplier must meet any relevant state licensure requirements under a statutory requirement pertaining to all Medicare DMEPOS suppliers inside and outside of the competitive bidding program, as well as regulatory requirements about the timing of when state licensure requirements need to be met for suppliers competing in a competitive bidding program; and each supplier must adhere to other criteria to ascertain whether their bids are bona fide and whether the supplier can provide the items based on the bids submitted.

For all suppliers that pass the non-price competition criteria, CMS arrays their composite bids from lowest to highest, and offers contracts to the suppliers with the lowest bids until enough suppliers have been offered contracts to more than supply the market. Suppliers can accept or reject the contract offers without penalty. Over 90% of suppliers who are offered Medicare contracts accept them.

The Medicare price or *single payment amount* for a competitively bid item is set at the median (or middle) bid for that item among all winning suppliers. This means that for half of the winning suppliers, the single payment amount will be less than the bid they submitted for that item, and for half of the suppliers, the single payment amount will be greater than their bid for that item.

Some have expressed concern that, since there is no penalty for rejecting a contract offer under the competitive bidding program, suppliers have an incentive to place low bids and then reject the contract when the single payment amounts (based in part on their own bids) are lower than they would prefer.

H.R. 2 would add specifically to the competitive acquisition statutes the requirement that suppliers meet applicable state licensure as an additional condition for being awarded a contract under the competitive bidding program.

H.R. 2 would require suppliers bidding for contracts that are to begin not earlier than January 1, 2017, and not later than January 1, 2019, to obtain bid bonds. The suppliers would be required to provide proof of the bid bonds to the Secretary. The bonds would be required to be between $50,000 and $100,000 for each competitive bidding area the supplier competes in. If a supplier were to be offered a contract for a category of DMEPOS in an area, the supplier's composite bid for the category was less than the median composite bid, and the supplier rejected the contract, the bond submitted by the supplier would be forfeited; and the Secretary would then be required to collect on the bond. In all other circumstances, the bond would be required to be returned to the suppliers within 90 days of the announcement of the winning suppliers. The Comptroller General would be required to evaluate the effect of the bid bond requirement on the participation of small suppliers and report the results of the study to Congress not later than six months after the date the first contracts subject to this requirement are awarded.

Section 523: Payment for Global Surgical Packages

Under the Medicare physician fee schedule, physicians receive a global payment for surgical services that covers preoperative and postoperative care provided immediately before and after the surgical procedure during the *global period*. There are three global packages: (1) 0-day global codes include the surgical procedure and the preoperative and postoperative physicians' services on the day of the procedure, including visits related to the service; (2) 10-day global codes include these services as well as visits related to the procedure during the 10 days following the procedure; and (3) 90-day global codes include the same services as the 0-day global codes plus the preoperative services furnished 1 day prior to the procedure and postoperative services during the 90 days immediately following the day of the procedure.

Because the payment rates and global packages were defined and based on data collected many years ago, the accuracy of the payments is uncertain and unlikely to reflect changes in standards of practice and newer technology. In the 2015 Medicare Physician Fee Schedule Final Rule, CMS proposed to redefine bundles by transitioning to 0-day global codes over several years and eliminating all 10- and 90-day global codes; medically reasonable and necessary visits would be billed and paid separately during the preoperative and postoperative periods outside of the day of the surgical procedure.

H.R. 2 would prohibit the implementation of this rule regarding global surgical packages and require the Secretary to collect data on services included in global surgical packages from a representative sample of physicians for the purpose of valuing surgical services, beginning no later than January 1, 2017. The information would include the number and level of medical visits and other items and services related to the surgery and furnished during the global services period, as appropriate, and would be reported on claims at the end of the global period or in another manner specified by the Secretary. CMS would receive $2 million from the Medicare Part B Trust Fund for FY2015 to implement this initiative, with funds to remain available until expended. The Secretary would reassess the value of the information collected every four years and could discontinue the data collection if adequate information on valuing surgical services were to be available from other sources such as qualified clinical data registries, surgical logs, billing systems or other practice or facility records, and electronic health records.

Beginning with 2019, the Secretary would use the information reported above together with other available data to improve the accuracy of valuation of surgical services under the Medicare physician fee schedule. The Secretary could delay 5% of the 10- or 90- day global payment as an incentive for physicians to report the required information. The HHS Inspector General would audit a sample of the information reported to verify the accuracy of the information.

Section 524: Extension of Secure Rural Schools and Community Self-Determination Act of 2000

Counties with national forest lands managed by the United States Forest Service and with certain Bureau of Land Management lands historically have received a percentage of agency revenues, primarily from timber sales.[61] However, timber sales declined substantially beginning in the 1990s, which led to significantly reduced payments to the counties. Thus, Congress enacted the Secure Rural Schools and Community Self-Determination Act of 2000 (SRS; P.L. 106-393)[62] as a temporary, optional program of payments based in part on historic rather than current revenues.[63] Authorization of mandatory spending for SRS payments originally expired at the end of FY2006, but the program was extended through FY2013 by several reauthorizations. SRS payments are disbursed after the end of each fiscal year, so the FY2013 SRS payment—the last authorized payment—was made in FY2014. County payments have returned to the revenue-based system that was in place before SRS. The FY2014 payment to counties—made in February 2015—was significantly lower than the previous years' SRS payments.

This provision would reauthorize mandatory spending for SRS payments for two years, at 95% of the funding level for the preceding fiscal year. The FY2014 payment, to be made within 45 days of enactment, would take into account the revenue-sharing payment that already has been disbursed to the counties.

Section 525: Exclusion from PAYGO Scorecards

H.R. 2 includes a provision preventing the bill's budgetary effects from being recorded on scorecards associated with statutory PAYGO and Senate PAYGO (*PAYGO* is often used interchangeably with the term *pay-as-you-go*). Both statutory and Senate PAYGO are budget enforcement mechanisms created with the goal of preventing new direct spending and revenue legislation from resulting in a projected net deficit increase.

In the case of statutory PAYGO, the Office of Management and Budget (OMB) maintains two PAYGO scorecards, covering rolling 5-year and 10-year periods. When legislation affecting direct spending or revenue is enacted, the projected net budgetary effect of the legislation is required to be recorded on the scorecards. At the end of a congressional session, OMB determines if the projected budgetary effects of all legislation recorded on the PAYGO scorecards will result in a net deficit increase for either time period. If it does, the President must issue a sequestration order that implements across-the-board cuts to nonexempt programs in an amount sufficient to remedy the projected deficit increase.[64] Section 525 of H.R. 2 directs that the measure's projected budgetary effects not be recorded on OMB's scorecards and therefore will not be factored into OMB's annual evaluation of the budgetary effects of enacted direct spending and revenue legislation.

In the case of Senate PAYGO, the rule prohibits consideration in the Senate of direct spending or revenue legislation that would increase the deficit over either a 6-year or 11-year period. A scorecard is maintained in the Senate that records the budgetary effects of such legislation. This scorecard, also referred to as a ledger, allows for the budgetary effects of any deficit reduction legislation enacted since the beginning of the calendar year to be used as an offset in the consideration of subsequent direct spending or revenue legislation.[65] Section 525 of H.R. 2 directs that the measure's budgetary effects will not be recorded on the Senate PAYGO scorecard and therefore will not affect the scorecard's current balance.

APPENDIX. LIST OF ABBREVIATIONS

ACA: The Patient Protection and Affordable Care Act (P.L. 111-148, as amended)
ACF: Administration for Children and Families
ADRC: Aging and Disability Resource Center
ARRA: The American Recovery and Reinvestment Act of 2009 (P.L. 111-5)
ATRA: The American Taxpayer Relief Act of 2012 (P.L. 112-240)
BBA97: The Balanced Budget Act of 1997 (P.L. 105-33)
BIPA: Benefits Improvement and Protection Act of 2000 (P.L. 106-554)
CAH: Critical access hospital
CERT: Comprehensive error rate testing
CHIP: State Children's Health Insurance Program
CHIPRA: Children's Health Insurance Program Reauthorization Act (P.L. 111-3)
CMS: Centers for Medicare & Medicaid Services
CPI-U: Consumer price index for all urban consumers
DME: Durable medical equipment

DMEPOS: Durable medical equipment, prosthetics, orthotics, and supplies
DRA: Deficit Reduction Act of 2005 (P.L. 109-171)
DSH: Disproportionate share hospital
FFS: Fee-for-service
FPL: Federal poverty level
FSA: The Family Support Act of 1988 (P.L. 100-485)
GAO: Government Accountability Office
GPCI: Geographic practice cost index
HCFAC: Health care fraud and abuse control
HHA: Home health agency
HHS: Department of Health & Human Services
HIPAA: Health Insurance Portability and Accountability Act of 1996 (P.L. 109-141)
JCT: Joint Committee on Taxation
LTCH: Long-term care hospital
MA: Medicare Advantage
MAC: Medicare administrative contractor
MAGI: Modified adjusted gross income
MA-PD: Medicare Advantage plans with a prescription drug component
MedPAC: Medicare Payment Advisory Commission
MCTRJCA: Middle Class Tax Relief and Job Creation Act of 2012 (P.L. 112-96)
MIECHV: Maternal, infant, and early childhood home visiting
MIPPA: Medicare Improvements for Patients and Providers Act of 2008 (P.L. 110-275)
MMA: Medicare Prescription Drug, Improvement, and Modernization Act of 2003 (P.L. 108- 173)
MMEA: Medicare and Medicaid Extenders Act of 2010 (P.L. 111-309)
MMSEA: Medicare, Medicaid and SCHIP Extension Act of 2007 (P.L. 110-173)
NPI: National provider identifier
OAA: Older Americans Act (P.L. 89-73, as amended)
OIG: The Department of Health and Human Services Office of Inspector General
OMB: Office of Management and Budget
PAMA: Protecting Access to Medicare Act of 2014 (P.L. 113-93)
PAYGO: Pay-as-you-go
PDE: Prescription drug event

PHSA: Public Health Service Act (P.L. 78-410)
PREP: Personal responsibility education program
PRWORA: Personal Responsibility and Work Opportunity Reconciliation Act of 1996 (P.L. 104- 193)
PSRA: Pathway for SGR Reform Act of 2013 (P.L. 113-67)
QI: Qualifying individual
RAC: Recovery audit contractor
SGR: Sustainable growth rate
SNF: Skilled nursing facility
SRS: Secure Rural Schools and Community Self-Determination Act of 2000 (P.L. 106-393)
SSA: Social Security Act
TEFRA: Tax Equity and Fiscal Responsibility Act of 1982 (P.L. 97-248)
TRHCA: Tax Relief and Health Care Act of 2006 (P.L. 109-432)
TMA: Transitional medical assistance

End Notes

[1] The estimates can be found at http://www.cbo.gov/sites/default/files/cbofiles/attachments/hr2.pdf.

[2] U.S. Government Accountability Office (GAO), *Clinical Data Registries: HHS Could Improve Medicare Quality and Efficiency through Key Requirements and Oversight*, GAO-14-75, December 2013, at http://www.gao.gov/assets/660/ 659701.pdf.

[3] The American Recovery and Reinvestment Act of 2009 (ARRA; P.L. 111-5) gave states the option to waive the requirement that individuals be enrolled in Medicaid for three out of the past six months in order to qualify for transitional medical assistance (TMA).

[4] ARRA gave states the option to waive the requirements for TMA enrollees in the second six-month period (i.e., requirements to report earnings and child care and to remain below 185% of the federal poverty level).

[5] For more information on the National Institutes of Health, see CRS Report R41705, *The National Institutes of Health (NIH): Background and Congressional Issues*, by Judith A. Johnson.

[6] For more information on the Indian Health Service (IHS), see CRS Report R43330, *The Indian Health Service (IHS): An Overview*, by Elayne J. Heisler.

[7] IHS-funded facilities refer to facilities operated directly by the IHS, by an Indian tribe, a tribal organization, or an urban Indian organization as these terms are defined in §4 of the Indian Health Care Improvement Act (25 U.S.C. §1604).

[8] For more information on abstinence education programs in Title V of the SSA, see CRS Report RS20301, *Teenage Pregnancy Prevention: Statistics and Programs*, by Carmen Solomon-Fears.

[9] For more information on the Maternal and Child Health Block Grant, see CRS Report R42428, *The Maternal and Child Health Services Block Grant: Background and Funding*, by Carmen Solomon-Fears.

[10] For more information, see CRS Report R43930, *Maternal and Infant Early Childhood Home Visiting (MIECHV) Program: Background and Funding*, by Adrienne L. Fernandes-Alcantara.

[11] For more information about Medicaid disproportionate share hospital payments, see CRS Report R42865, *Medicaid Disproportionate Share Hospital Payments*, by Alison Mitchell.

[12] Arkansas Dept. of Health and Human Services v. Ahlborn and Wos v. E.M.A.

[13] For more information on health centers, see CRS Report R43937, *Federal Health Centers: An Overview*, by Elayne J. Heisler.

[14] For more information on the National Health Service Corps, see CRS Report R43920, *National Health Service Corps: Changes in Funding and Impact on Recruitment*, by Bernice Reyes-Akinbileje.

[15] Specifically, these sections of P.L. 113-235 state

(a) None of the funds appropriated in this Act, and none of the funds in any trust fund to which funds are appropriated in this Act, shall be expended for any abortion. (b) None of the funds appropriated in this Act, and none of the funds in any trust fund to which funds are appropriated in this Act, shall be expended for health benefits coverage that includes coverage of abortion. (c) The term "health benefits coverage" means the package of services covered by a managed care provider or organization pursuant to a contract or other arrangement. §507. (a) The limitations established in the preceding section shall not apply to an abortion—(1) if the pregnancy is the result of an act of rape or incest; or (2) in the case where a woman suffers from a physical disorder, physical injury, or physical illness, including a life-endangering physical condition caused by or arising from the pregnancy itself, that would, as certified by a physician, place the woman in danger of death unless an abortion is performed. (b) Nothing in the preceding section shall be construed as prohibiting the expenditure by a State, locality, entity, or private person of State, local, or private funds (other than a State's or locality's contribution of Medicaid matching funds). (c) Nothing in the preceding section shall be construed as restricting the ability of any managed care provider from offering abortion coverage or the ability of a State or locality to contract separately with such a provider for such coverage with State funds (other than a State's or locality's contribution of Medicaid matching funds). (d)(1) None of the funds made available in this Act may be made available to a Federal agency or program, or to a State or local government, if such agency, program, or government subjects any institutional or individual health care entity to discrimination on the basis that the health care entity does not provide, pay for, provide coverage of, or refer for abortions. (2) In this subsection, the term "health care entity" includes an individual physician or other health care professional, a hospital, a provider-sponsored organization, a health maintenance organization, a health insurance plan, or any other kind of health care facility, organization, or plan.

[16] For more information about CHIP financing, see CRS Report R43949, *Federal Financing for the State Children's Health Insurance Program (CHIP)*, by Alison Mitchell.

[17] This penalty is the same as that currently imposed on entities who knowingly sell health insurance policies to Medicare beneficiaries that duplicate existing health care coverage. (Social Security Act §1882(d)(3)(A).)

[18] The Medicare Prescription Drug, Improvement, and Modernization Act of 2003 (MMA; P.L. 108-173) would have phased in the increase over five years; however, the Deficit Reduction Act of 2005 (DRA; P.L. 109-171) shortened the phase-in period to three years.

[19] In 2015, the standard monthly Part B premium is $104.90. For additional information on Part B premiums, see CRS Report R40082, *Medicare: Part B Premiums*, by Patricia A. Davis.

[20] In 2015, the base monthly Part D premium is $33.13; however, actual premiums paid by beneficiaries may vary depending on the prescription drug plan that they select. See CRS Report R40611, *Medicare Part D Prescription Drug Benefit*, by Suzanne M. Kirchhoff and Patricia A. Davis.

[21] §3402 of the ACA.

[22] For more information about Medicaid disproportionate share hospital payments, see CRS Report R42865, *Medicaid Disproportionate Share Hospital Payments*, by Alison Mitchell.

[23] GAO, *Medicare: CMS Needs an Approach and a Reliable Cost Estimate for Removing Social Security Numbers from Medicare Cards*, GAO-12-831, August 2012.

[24] Centers for Medicare & Medicaid Service (CMS), *SSN Removal from Medicare Card: Cost Analysis Summary*, May 10, 2013, at http://waysandmeans.house.gov/uploadedfiles/ssn_removal_revised_report_final_5-10-2013.pdf.

[25] Incarcerated individuals include "individuals who are under arrest, incarcerated, imprisoned, escaped from confinement, under supervised release, on medical furlough, required to reside in mental health facilities, required to reside in halfway houses, required to live under home detention, or confined completely or partially in any way under a penal statute or rule."

[26] U.S. Department of Health and Human Services (HHS), Office of the Inspector General (OIG), *Medicare Improperly Paid Providers Millions of Dollars for Incarcerated Beneficiaries Who Received Services During 2009 Through 2011*, A-07-12-01113, January 2013.

[27] HHS, OIG, *Medicare Paid for HIV Drugs for Deceased BeneficiariesI,* OEI-02-11-00172, October 2014.

[28] HHS, OIG, *Medicare Improperly Paid Millions of Dollars for Prescription Drugs Provided to Unlawfully Present Beneficiaries During 2009 through 2011*, A-07-12-06038, October 2013.

[29] Under Medicare Parts C and D, private health plans provide services to beneficiaries. Most health plans issue their own identification cards to beneficiaries that do not contain Social Security numbers (SSNs). Health insurance claim numbers are 10- or 11-digits including the 9-digit SSN and a beneficiary identifier assigned to the beneficiary and other dependents.

[30] CMS, *SSN Removal from Medicare Card: Cost Analysis Summary*, May 10, 2013, at http://waysandmeans.house.gov/uploadedfiles/ssn_removal_revised_report_final_5-10-2013.pdf.

[31] GAO, *Medicare Information Technology: Centers for Medicare & Medicaid Services Needs to Pursue a Solution for Removing Social Security Numbers from Cards*, GAO-13-761, September 2013.

[32] As presented by a GAO report required by the conference report to accompany the Consolidated Appropriations Act, 2014 (P.L. 113-76).

[33] CMS, *Recovery Auditing in Medicare and Medicaid for Fiscal Year 2013*, at http://www.cms.gov/ResearchStatistics-Data-and-Systems/Monitoring-Programs/Medicare-FFS-Compliance-Programs/Recovery-Audit-Program/ Downloads/FY-2013-Report-To-Congress.pdf.

[34] The additional functions that might be required of Medicare administrative contractors include activities to support the Medicare Integrity Program under SSA §1893.

[35] CMS, *Medicare Prescription Drug Benefit Manual*, Chapter 9, Compliance Program Guidelines, Section 50, Elements of an Effective Compliance Program, at http://www.cms.gov/Medicare/Prescription-Drug-Coverage/PrescriptionDrugCovContra/Downloads/Chapter9.pdf.

[36] HHS, OIG, *Invalid Prescriber Identifiers on Medicare Part D Drug Claims*, OEI-03-09-00140, June 2010.

[37] For more information, see https://www.mymedicare.gov/.

[38] CMS began the acquisition process in November 2005. The first round of Medicare administrative contractor (MAC) procurements included all procurements completed or in progress of as of September 1, 2010.

[39] For more information, see http://www.cms.gov/Medicare/Medicare-Contracting/Medicare-AdministrativeContractors/Vision-of-Future-Fee-for-Service-Medicare-Environment.html.

[40] CMS, *CMS to Delay Further Medicare Administrative Contractor (MAC) Jurisdiction Consolidations*, March 19, 2014, at http://www.cms.gov/Medicare/Medicare-Contracting/Medicare-Administrative-Contractors/Downloads/RFIAnnouncement-AB-MAC-March-2014.pdf.

[41] HHS, OIG, *Medicare Administrative Contractors' Performance*, OEI-03-11-00740, January 2014.

[42] SSA §1874A(b)(1)(B).

[43] Effective September 3, 2014, the CMS contracting officer can exercise options only after determining the contractor's performance on the contract was acceptable (received satisfactory ratings), 78 *Federal Register* 46783, August 1, 2013.

[44] HHS, OIG, *Medicare Administrative Contractors' Performance,* OEI-03-11-00740, January 2014.

[45] CMS founded the California Medicare and Medicaid Data Analysis Center (CMMDAC) on September 28, 2001, to show proof of concept for dual Medicare-Medicaid data analysis. CMMDAC was established to demonstrate the value of comparative Medicare-Medicaid claims data analysis for the detection, prosecution, and elimination of aberrant practices, Medicaid Alliance for Program Safeguards, May 2005.

[46] Texas, Illinois, Pennsylvania, North Carolina, New Jersey, Ohio, and Washington had agreed to participate in the Medi-Medi pilot in 2005.

[47] HHS, OIG, *The Medicare-Medicaid (Medi-Medi) Data Match Program*, OEI-09-08-00370, April 2012.

[48] In 2008, the following 10 states were participating in the Medi-Medi program: California, Florida, Illinois, New Jersey, New York, North Carolina, Ohio, Pennsylvania, Texas, and Washington.

[49] Under the Medi-Medi program, the Secretary has authority to waive only such requirements of SSA Title XVIII, and Titles XI and XIX as are necessary to carry out the Medi-Medi program (SSA §1893(g)(2)).

[50] GAO, "Clinical Data Registries: HHS Could Improve Medicare Quality and Efficiency through Key Requirements and Oversight," December 2013, at http://www.gao.gov/assets/660/659701.pdf.

[51] 42 U.S.C. §1320a-7a. Civil penalties do not apply to beneficiaries under this provision. Under 42 U.S.C. §1320a7a(i)(5), a beneficiary is defined as an individual who is eligible to receive items or services for which payment may be made under a federal health care program, but excludes any providers, suppliers, or practitioners. However, it may be noted that beneficiaries still may be subject to criminal penalties under 42 U.S.C. §1320a-7b.

[52] For more information on Medicare home health services, see CRS Report R42998, *Medicare Home Health Benefit Primer: Benefit Basics and Issues*, by Scott R. Talaga.

[53] HHS, OIG, *Surety Bonds Remain an Unused Tool to Protect Medicare from Home Health Overpayments*, OEI-03- 12-00070, September 2012.

[54] CMS, *Medicare Benefit Policy Manual*, Chapter 15, Subluxation May be Demonstrated by X-Ray or Physician's Exam, §240.1.2, defines subluxation as "A motion segment, in which alignment, movement integrity, and/or physiological function of the spine are altered although contact between joint surfaces remains intact."

[55] Medicare does not cover maintenance chiropractic care. If no further improvement in a beneficiary's condition can be expected, then continuing, maintenance, chiropractic care would not be covered by Medicare.

[56] OIG, *Inappropriate Medicare Payments for Chiropractic Services*, OEI-07-07-00390, May 2009.

[57] CMS defines *medical review* as the collection of information and clinical review of medical records by Medicare Contractors to ensure that payment is made only for services that meet all Medicare coverage, coding, and medical necessity requirements, at http://www.cms.gov/Research-Statistics-Data-and-Systems/Monitoring-Programs/MedicareFFS-Compliance-Programs/Medical-Review/.

[58] Medicare's general medical necessity requirements are available at SSA §1862(a)(1)(A).

[59] See CRS Report RL 33587, *Medicare Secondary Payer, Coordination of Benefits* by Suzanne Kirchhoff.

[60] HHS, *Department of Health and Human Services Agency Financial Report*: *FY2014*, November 2014, p. 23, at http://www.hhs.gov/afr/fy2014-mda.pdf.

[61] Act of May 23, 1908, 16 U.S.C. §500 (directing that 25% of the gross revenue generated on national forest system lands is returned to the counties containing those lands for the "benefit of public schools and public roads"), and the Act of August 28, 1937, ch. 876, 43 U.S.C. §§1181a-1181j (directing that 50% of the revenue generated on certain lands in Oregon is returned to the counties containing those lands, to be used for any governmental purpose). For more information see CRS Report R42951, *The Oregon and California Railroad Lands (O&C Lands): Issues for Congress*, by Katie Hoover.

[62] P.L. 106-393, 16 U.S.C. §§7101-7153. For more information, see CRS Report R41303, *Reauthorizing the Secure Rural Schools and Community Self-Determination Act of 2000*, by Katie Hoover.

[63] The payment formula to determine a county's payment is based half on the revenues generated between FY1986 and FY1999 and half on the proportion of agency land within the county, with an adjustment factor based on relative county income.

[64] For more information on statutory PAYGO, see CRS Report R41157, *The Statutory Pay-As-You-Go Act of 2010: Summary and Legislative History*, by Bill Heniff Jr.

[65] For more information on the Senate PAYGO rule, see CRS Report RL31943, *Budget Enforcement Procedures: Senate Pay-As-You-Go (PAYGO) Rule*, by Bill Heniff Jr.

In: State Children's Health Insurance Program
Editor: Marty Sparks
ISBN: 978-1-63483-675-3

Chapter 3

FEDERAL FINANCING FOR THE STATE CHILDREN'S HEALTH INSURANCE PROGRAM (CHIP)*

Alison Mitchell

SUMMARY

The State Children's Health Insurance Program (CHIP) is a means-tested program that provides health coverage to targeted low-income children and pregnant women in families that have annual income above Medicaid eligibility levels but have no health insurance. CHIP is jointly financed by the federal government and the states, and the states are responsible for administering CHIP.

The federal government pays about 70% of CHIP expenditures, and the federal government's share of CHIP expenditures (including both services and administration) is determined by the enhanced federal medical assistance percentage (E-FMAP) rate. In FY2015, the E-FMAP rate ranges from 65% (13 states) to 82% (Mississippi). The Patient Protection and Affordable Care Act (ACA; P.L. 111-148, as amended) included a provision to increase the E-FMAP rate by 23 percentage points for most CHIP expenditures from FY2016 through FY2019.

---

* This is an edited, reformatted and augmented version of a Congressional Research Service publication R43949 , prepared for Members and Committees of Congress dated April 23, 2015.

The federal appropriation for CHIP is provided in statute. From this federal appropriation, states receive CHIP allotments, which are the federal funds allocated to each state and the territories for the federal share of their CHIP expenditures. In addition, if a state has a shortfall in federal CHIP funding, there are a few sources of shortfall funding, such as the Child Enrollment Contingency Fund, redistribution funds, and Medicaid funds.

FY2015 was the final year for which federal CHIP funding was provided in statute, but the Medicare Access and CHIP Reauthorization Act of 2015 (MACRA; P.L. 114-10) extended federal CHIP funding, among other provisions. Specifically, P.L. 114-10 extended CHIP funding for two additional years (i.e., through FY2017) and maintained the current allotment formula with the 23 percentage point increase to the E-FMAP. The bill also extended the qualifying state option, the Child Enrollment Contingency Fund, and outreach and enrollment grants.

With FY2017 now being the final year for which federal CHIP funding is provided in statute, Congress's action or inaction over the next couple of years will determine the future of CHIP and of health coverage for CHIP children. In considering the future of CHIP, Congress has a number of policy options, including extending federal CHIP funding and continuing the program or letting CHIP funding expire.

Even though federal CHIP funding is set to expire after FY2017, under current law the ACA maintenance of effort (MOE) requirement for children is in place through FY2019. The MOE provision requires states to maintain income eligibility levels for CHIP children through September 30, 2019, as a condition for receiving federal Medicaid payments (notwithstanding the lack of corresponding federal CHIP appropriations for FY2018 and FY2019). If federal CHIP funding expires, the MOE requirement would impact CHIP Medicaid expansion programs and separate CHIP programs differently. States with CHIP Medicaid expansion programs must continue to cover their CHIP children once federal funding is no longer available. However, states with separate CHIP programs would not be required to continue coverage.

This report provides an overview of CHIP financing, beginning with an explanation of the federal matching rate. It describes various aspects of federal CHIP funding, such as the federal appropriation, state allotments, the Child Enrollment Contingency Fund, redistribution funds, outreach and enrollment grants, and performance bonus payments. The report ends with a section about the future of CHIP funding, including the options for extending CHIP funding and what could happen if federal funding expires.

INTRODUCTION

The State Children's Health Insurance Program (CHIP) is a federal-state program that provides health coverage to certain uninsured, low-income children and pregnant women in families that have annual income above Medicaid eligibility levels but do not have health insurance.[1] CHIP is jointly financed by the federal government and the states and is administered by the states. Participation in CHIP is voluntary, and all states and the District of Columbia participate. The federal government sets basic requirements for CHIP, but states have the flexibility to design their own version of CHIP within the federal government's basic framework. As a result, there is significant variation across CHIP programs.

States may design their CHIP programs in one of three ways: a CHIP Medicaid expansion, a separate CHIP program, or a combination approach in which the state operates a CHIP Medicaid expansion and one or more separate CHIP programs concurrently. CHIP benefit coverage and cost-sharing rules depend on program design. CHIP Medicaid expansions must follow the federal Medicaid rules for benefits and cost sharing. For separate CHIP programs, the benefits are permitted to look more like private health insurance and states may impose cost sharing, such as premiums or enrollment fees, with a maximum allowable amount that is tied to annual family income.

FY2017 is the last year federal CHIP funding has been appropriated in statute even though the Patient Protection and Affordable Care Act's (ACA; P.L. 111-148, as amended) maintenance of effort (MOE) requirement is in place through FY2019.[2] The ACA MOE provision requires states to maintain income eligibility levels for CHIP children through September 30, 2019, as a condition for receiving federal Medicaid payments (notwithstanding the lack of corresponding federal CHIP appropriations for FY2018 and FY2019).

This report provides an overview of CHIP financing, beginning with an explanation of the federal matching rate. It describes various aspects of federal CHIP funding, such as the federal appropriation, state allotments, the Child Enrollment Contingency Fund, redistribution funds, outreach and enrollment grants, and performance bonus payments. The report ends with a section about the future of CHIP funding, including the options for extending CHIP funding and what could happen if federal funding expires.

Federal Matching Rate

The federal government pays about 70% of CHIP expenditures, and the federal government's share of CHIP expenditures (including both services and administration) is determined by the enhanced federal medical assistance percentage (E-FMAP) rate.

The E-FMAP rate is based on the FMAP rate, which is the federal matching rate for the Medicaid program. The FMAP formula compares each state's average per capita income with average U.S. per capita income. The formula provides higher reimbursement to states with lower incomes (with a statutory maximum of 83%) and lower reimbursement to states with higher incomes (with a statutory minimum of 50%).

The E-FMAP rate is calculated by reducing the state share under the regular FMAP rate by 30.0%.[3] Statutorily, the E-FMAP (or federal matching rate) can range from 65.0% to 85.0%.[4] In FY2015, the E-FMAP ranges from 65.0% (13 states) to 81.5% (Mississippi).

For some CHIP expenditures, the federal matching rate is different than the E-FMAP rate. For instance, the matching rate for translation and interpretation services is the higher of 75% or states' E-FMAP rate plus 5 percentage points. Also, the Children's Health Insurance Program Reauthorization Act (CHIPRA; P.L. 111-3) included a provision that reduced the matching rate to the regular FMAP rate for children with family incomes exceeding 300% of the federal poverty level (FPL) with an exception for certain states.[5]

The ACA included a provision to increase the E-FMAP rate by 23 percentage points (not to exceed 100%) for most CHIP expenditures from FY2016 through FY2019. The 23 percentage point increase will not apply to certain expenditures, such as translation services, CHIP children above 300% of FPL (with an exception for certain states), expenditures for administration of citizenship documentation requirements, expenditures for administration of payment error rate measurement (PERM), and Medicaid coverage of certain breast or cervical cancer patients.

This provision will increase the statutory range of the E-FMAP rate to between 88% and 100%. In FY2016, 12 states are expected to have E-FMAP rates of 100%. Figure 1 shows the state distribution of E-FMAP rates for FY2016 with the 23 percentage point increase. Because the federal share of CHIP will be significantly higher with this increase, states are expected to spend through the federal CHIP funding allocated to them (i.e., state CHIP allotments) faster when the enhanced rate takes effect.

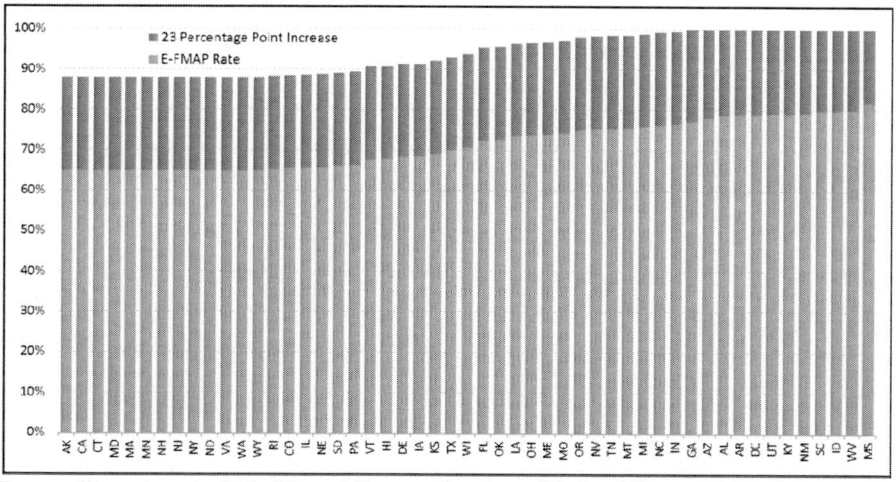

Source: Department of Health and Human Services, "Federal Financial Participation in State Assistance Expenditures; Federal Matching Shares for Medicaid, the Children's Health Insurance Program, and Aid to Needy Aged, Blind, or Disabled Persons for October 1, 2015 Through September 30, 2016," 79 Federal Register 71426, December 2, 2014.

Note: E-FMAP = Enhanced federal medical assistance percentage.

Figure 1. State Distribution of E-FMAP Rate with the 23 Percentage Point Increase (FY2016).

FEDERAL CHIP FUNDING

Federal CHIP funding is mandatory spending (i.e., funding controlled outside of the annual appropriations process through authorizing laws), and this funding is an entitlement to states that adhere to the federal CHIP rules. The funding for this program is provided through a mandatory appropriation set in statute.

Figure 2 shows the federal appropriation amounts and federal expenditures for CHIP from FY1998 through FY2014. The national appropriation amount is the maximum amount of federal funding for CHIP. Most of the federal CHIP expenditures are from state CHIP allotments, which are the federal funds allocated to each state to finance its CHIP program. In addition to allotments, states could receive shortfall funding, such as Child Enrollment Contingency Fund payments, redistribution funds, or Medicaid funds. Some CHIP funding is used to finance some Medicaid expenses. Also, states can receive outreach and enrollment grants, and states were eligible for performance bonus payments from FY2009 through FY2013.

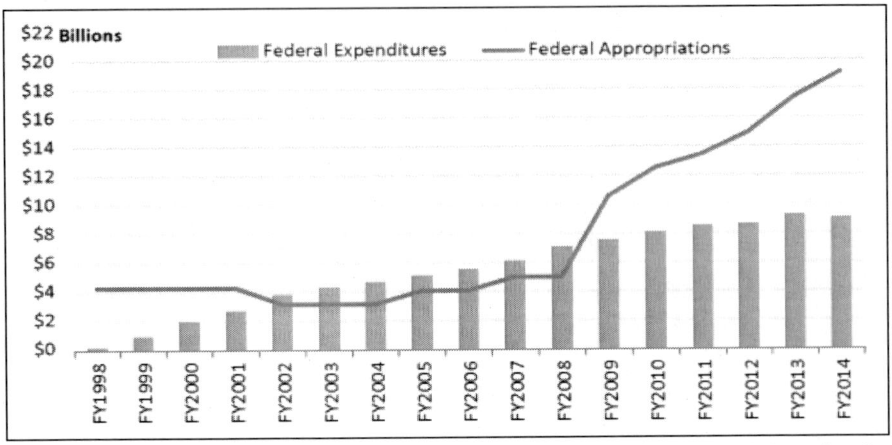

Sources: Appropriated amounts are from §2104 and §2105 of the Social Security Act and §108 of the Children's Health Insurance Program eauthorization Act (CHIPRA, P.L. 111-3) as amended by §10203(d)(2)(F) of the Patient Protection and Affordable Care Act (ACA; P.L. 111-148, as amended); and Medicaid Financial Management Reports.

Figure 2. CHIP Federal Expenditures and Federal Appropriations (FY1998 through FY2014).

Federal Appropriation

The federal appropriation for CHIP is provided in Section 2104(a) of the Social Security Act. This amount is the overall annual ceiling on federal CHIP spending to the states, the District of Columbia, and the territories.[6] CHIPRA increased the annual appropriation amounts substantially beginning in FY2009 and provided funding through FY2013. The ACA provided funding for an additional two years (i.e., through FY2015), and the Medicare Access and CHIP Reauthorization Act of 2015 (MACRA; P.L. 114-10) added appropriations for FY2016 and FY2017 at $19.3 billion and $20.4 billion,[7] respectively.[8]

If the federal appropriations were not large enough to cover state allotments in any given year, the state allotments would be reduced proportionally. However, Figure 2 shows the national appropriation has been more than sufficient to fund federal CHIP expenditures since FY2009.[9]

CHIP Changes in Mandatory Programs

Changes in mandatory programs (CHIMPs) are provisions in appropriations acts that reduce or constrain mandatory spending. From FY2011 through FY2015, multiple appropriations laws have rescinded a total of $24.3 billion in funding from CHIP through CHIMPs directed at the performance bonus payments fund.

CHIPRA established performance bonus payments for states that increase their Medicaid (not CHIP) enrollment among low-income children above a defined baseline (see the "Performance Bonus Payments" section). Funding for the performance bonus payments was provided through an initial, one-time appropriation of $3.2 billion in FY2009. In addition, funding for the bonus payments was transferred annually from unobligated federal appropriations for FY2009 through FY2013, excess funding in the Child Enrollment Contingency Fund for FY2009 through FY2013, and unexpended state allotments not used for redistribution for FY2009 through FY2013.

The fund balance for the performance bonus payments increased significantly every year because the transfers into the fund were substantially higher than the actual performance bonus payments to states. From FY2009 through FY2013, 27 states received CHIPRA performance bonus payments totaling $1.1 billion over the 5 years. Table 1 shows the annual aggregate performance bonus payment amounts and the annual rescission amounts.

Table 1. Performance Bonus Fund Payments to States and Rescission Amounts ($ in billions)

	FY2009	FY2010	FY2011	FY2012	FY2013	FY2014	FY2015	Total
Payments to States	$0.0	-$0.2	-$0.3	-$0.3	-$0.3	—	—	-$1.1
Rescission Amounts	—	—	-$3.5	-$6.4	-$6.4	-$6.3	-$1.7	-$24.3

Sources: Centers for Medicare & Medicaid Services, CHIPRA Performance Bonuses: A History, December 2013; Defense and Full-Year Appropriations, 2011 (P.L. 112-10); Consolidated Appropriations Act, 2012 (P.L. 112-74); Consolidated and Further Continuing Appropriations Act, 2013, (P.L. 113-6); Consolidated Appropriations Act, 2014 (P.L. 113-76); and Consolidated and Further Continuing Appropriations Act, 2015 (P.L. 113-235).

Note: Performance bonus payments were $37 million in FY2009.

In fact, from FY2011 through FY2015, multiple appropriations laws have rescinded a total of $24.3 billion in funding from CHIP (see text box entitled "CHIP Changes in Mandatory Programs" for more detail about these rescissions).

State Allotments

State allotments are the federal funds allocated to each state and territory for the federal share of its CHIP expenditures. CHIPRA established a new allocation of federal CHIP funds among the states based largely on states' actual use of and projected need for CHIP funds.[10] There are two formulas for determining state allotments: an even-year formula and an odd-year formula.[11]

In even years, such as FY2014, state CHIP allotments are each state's *allotment* for the prior year plus any Child Enrollment Contingency Fund (described below) payments from the previous year adjusted for growth in per capita National Health Expenditures and child population in the state. For even years, the formula for CHIP allotments can be increased to reflect CHIP eligibility or benefit expansions.

In odd years, state CHIP allotments are each state's *spending* for the prior year (including federal CHIP payments from the state CHIP allotment, payments from the Child Enrollment Contingency Fund, and redistribution funds) adjusted using the same growth factor as the even-year formula (i.e., per capita National Health Expenditures growth and child population growth in the state). Since the odd-year formula is based on states' actual use of CHIP funds, it is called the *re-basing year* because a state's CHIP allotment can either increase or decrease depending on that state's CHIP expenditures in the previous year. Figure 3 shows how the re-basing for FY2011 significantly decreased the aggregate amount for state allotments from FY2010 to FY2011.

State CHIP allotment funds are available to states for two years, which explains why federal expenditures are sometimes higher than the state allotments in some years. The federal CHIP expenditures can include federal funding from states' allotments for the specified year and the prior year.

The allotment is available to states to cover the federal share of both CHIP benefit and administrative expenditures.[12] However, no more than 10% of the federal CHIP funds that a state draws down from its CHIP allotment can be spent on non-benefit expenditures, including expenditures for administration, translation services, and outreach efforts.

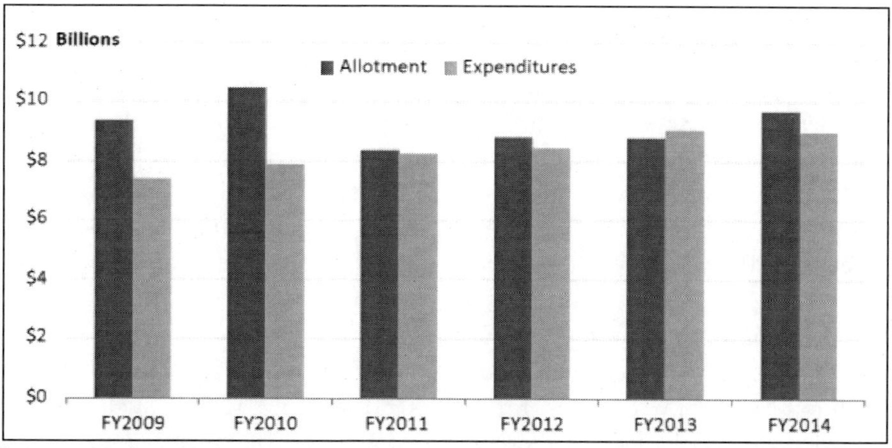

Sources: Various Federal Register notices; Chris Peterson and Ben Finder, Extending CHIP: Short-Term Issues, Medicaid and CHIP Payment and Access Commission, February 26, 2015.

Note: This figure does not show the availability of unspent allotments from the prior year and redistribution funds.

Figure 3. CHIP Allotments and Federal Expenditures (FY2009 through FY2014).

MACRA added a couple of special rules to the state allotments for FY2016 and FY2018. The special rule for FY2016 establishes the states' allotments by taking into account the 23 percentage point increase in the E-FMAP that begins in that year. Specifically, the FY2016 allotments will be each state's FY2015 allotment (including Child Enrollment Contingency Fund payments and redistribution funds), but it will be determined as if the 23 percentage point increase in the EFMAP were in place for FY2015. Then, that amount will be adjusted using the same growth factor as the even- and odd-year formulas (i.e., growth in per capita National Health Expenditures and child population in the state).

For FY2018, MACRA included a provision that will reduce the amount of states' unspent funds from their FY2017 allotments available for expenditures in FY2018 by one-third. Although FY2017 is the last year for which federal CHIP funding is provided under current law, states could have federal CHIP spending in FY2018 because states could have access to unspent funds from their FY2017 allotments and unspent FY2016 allotments redistributed to shortfall states.

Shortfall Funding

If a state's CHIP allotment for the current year, in addition to any allotment funds carried over from the prior year, is insufficient to cover the state's projected CHIP expenditures for the current year, a few different shortfall funding sources are available. These sources include the Child Enrollment Contingency Fund, redistribution funds, and Medicaid funds. Since FY2009, one state and one territory have received shortfall funding.

Child Enrollment Contingency Fund

CHIPRA established the Child Enrollment Contingency Fund and made its funds available to states for FY2009 through FY2015, and MACRA extended the availability of the Child Enrollment Contingency Fund and of payments from the fund through FY2017.[13] A state is eligible for Child Enrollment Contingency Fund payments if it has both a funding shortfall[14] and CHIP enrollment (for children) that exceeds a target level.[15] As a result, not all states with funding shortfalls are eligible for Child Enrollment Contingency Fund payments.

The Child Enrollment Contingency Fund was funded with an initial deposit equal to 20% of the appropriated amount for FY2009 (i.e., $2.1 billion). In addition, for FY2010 through FY2017, such sums as are necessary for making Child Enrollment Contingency Fund payments to eligible states are to be deposited into the fund, but these transfers cannot exceed 20% of the federal appropriation for the fiscal year.

The Child Enrollment Contingency Fund payment formula is based on a state's growth in CHIP enrollment and per capita spending, which means a state may receive a payment from the fund that does not equal its actual shortfall. Iowa is the only state that has received payments from the Child Enrollment Contingency Fund since FY2009, when funds were first available.[16]

Redistribution Funds

After two years, any unused state CHIP allotment funds are redistributed to shortfall states.[17] For redistribution funds, a shortfall state is defined as a state that will not have enough money to meet projected costs in the current year after counting (1) the current year's state allotment, (2) unspent funds from the prior year's state allotment, and (3) available Child Enrollment Contingency Fund payments. If redistributed funds are insufficient to meet the needs of all shortfall states, each shortfall state receives a proportionate share of the available funds based on the shortfall in each state. Since FY2009, only Puerto Rico has received redistribution funds.[18]

Medicaid Funds

States that design their CHIP program as a CHIP Medicaid expansion or a combination program and face a shortfall after receiving Child Enrollment Contingency Fund payments and redistribution funds may receive federal Medicaid matching funds to fund the shortfall in the CHIP Medicaid expansion portion of their CHIP program.[19] When Medicaid funds are used to fund CHIP, the state receives the lower regular FMAP rate (i.e., the federal Medicaid matching rate) rather than the higher E-FMAP rate provided for other CHIP expenditures. However, although federal CHIP funding is capped, federal Medicaid funding is open-ended, which means there is no upper limit or cap on the amount of federal Medicaid funds a state may receive.

Federal CHIP Funds Finance Some Medicaid Expenditures

In a few situations, federal CHIP funding is used to finance Medicaid expenditures, such as the *qualifying state* option, the stairstep children, and the transition to the modified adjusted gross income (MAGI) counting rules.

Qualifying State Option

Certain states had significantly expanded Medicaid eligibility for children prior to the enactment of CHIP in 1997, and these states are allowed to use their CHIP allotment funds to fund the difference between the Medicaid and CHIP matching rates (i.e., FMAP and E-FMAP rates, respectively) to finance the cost for children in Medicaid above 133% of FPL. This provision is referred to as the *qualifying state* option. FY2015 was the last year for which the qualifying state option was authorized, but MACRA extended the qualifying state option through FY2017.

The following 11 states meet the definition of a qualifying state: Connecticut, Hawaii, Maryland, Minnesota, New Hampshire, New Mexico, Rhode Island, Tennessee, Vermont, Washington, and Wisconsin. Although 11 states are eligible for this option, only 6 states (Connecticut, Minnesota, New Hampshire, Vermont, Washington, and Wisconsin) had CHIP expenditures under the qualifying state option in FY2013.

Stairstep Children

The ACA required states to transition CHIP children aged 6 through 18 in families with annual income less than 133% of FPL to Medicaid, beginning January 1, 2014.[20] Coverage for such children continues to be financed with states' CHIP annual allotment funding at the E-FMAP rate as long as their income eligibility is greater than the state's March 31, 1997, Medicaid income standard for children.[21] However, the E-FMAP rate is not available for children between the ages of 6 and 18 who have access to private health insurance.

Transition to Modified Adjusted Gross Income

Beginning January 1, 2014, the ACA required the federal government and states to rely on MAGI[22] income counting rules when determining eligibility for most CHIP enrollees. Under the MAGI rules, a state looks at each individual's MAGI, deducts 5% (which the law provides as a standard disregard), and compares that income with the new income standards set by each state.[23] Children moving from CHIP to Medicaid due to the application of the 5% income disregard may be funded with states' annual CHIP allotment funding at the E-FMAP rate.[24]

Outreach and Enrollment Grants

CHIPRA established outreach and enrollment grants aimed at reducing the number of children eligible for but not enrolled in Medicaid and CHIP and improving retention so that eligible children stay covered for as long as they are eligible for the programs. CHIPRA provided $100 million to fund the outreach and enrollment grants for FY2009 through FY2013. The ACA extended the outreach and enrollment grants through FY2015 and provided an additional $40 million in funding. MACRA extended the outreach and enrollment grants through FY2017 and authorized another $40 million in funding.

Ten percent of the allocation was to be directed to a national enrollment campaign, and 10% was to be targeted to outreach for American Indian and Alaska Native children. The remaining 80% was to be distributed among state and local governments and to community-based organizations for purposes of conducting outreach campaigns, with a particular focus on rural areas and underserved populations. Grant funds also were targeted at proposals that address cultural and linguistic barriers to enrollment.

Performance Bonus Payments

CHIPRA established performance bonus payments for states that increased their Medicaid (not CHIP) enrollment among low-income children above a defined baseline. CHIPRA performance bonus payments began in FY2009, and FY2013 was the final year in which a state could earn a bonus payment. To qualify for these bonus payments, states had to (1) implement strategies to simplify the application and enrollment process and (2) achieve state-specific targets for increasing Medicaid enrollment among children.

There were two tiers of bonus payments depending on how much the state's enrollment exceeded the baseline. Tier 1 bonus payments were available to states with enrollment exceeding the baseline by less than 10%, and tier 1 bonus payments were calculated by multiplying the amount the enrollment exceeded the baseline by 15% of the state-specific per capita Medicaid expenditures. States with enrollment exceeding the baseline enrollment level by more than 10% also received additional tier 2 bonus payments for the enrollment in excess of 10% above baseline, and Tier 2 bonus payments were calculated by multiplying the amount the enrollment exceeded the baseline plus 10% by 62.5% of the state-specific per capita Medicaid expenditures.

From FY2009 through FY2013, 27 states received CHIPRA performance bonus payments totaling $1.1 billion over the five years. Some states received payments in more than one year.[25] Funding for the performance bonus payments was provided through an initial one-time appropriation of $3.2 billion in FY2009. In addition, funding for these payments was transferred from unobligated national allotments for FY2009 through FY2013, excess funding in the Child Enrollment Contingency Fund for FY2010 through FY2013, and unexpended allotments not used for redistribution for FY2010 through FY2013.

Future of CHIP Funding

With federal funding for CHIP set to end after FY2017, Congress will need to decide whether to continue the program. In considering the future of CHIP, it is helpful to recall why the program was created in 1997: to provide affordable health coverage at a time when there were few other insurance coverage options for low-income children outside of Medicaid. The health insurance market is far different today, with the enactment of the ACA. Now, if CHIP funding is exhausted, current CHIP-eligible children could be eligible for Medicaid or potentially for subsidized coverage in the health insurance exchanges. However, not all CHIP-eligible children would be eligible for these programs, and some could end up being uninsured if CHIP is no longer available.

Some argue that it is important to continue providing CHIP children with child-specific safety net coverage because each of the low-income subsidy programs (e.g., CHIP, Medicaid, and subsidized exchange coverage) plays a unique role in the health care delivery system.[26] For instance, greater cost-sharing protections exist for the programs that target families at the lower ends of the income eligibility spectrum.[27] In addition, some are wary of providing coverage for children in the health insurance exchanges because the exchanges are new and there is little evidence about how coverage in the exchanges compares to CHIP coverage.[28]

With FY2017 being the final year for which federal CHIP funding is provided in statute, Congress's action or inaction will determine the future of CHIP and of health coverage for CHIP children. In considering the future of CHIP, Congress has a number of policy options, including extending federal CHIP funding and continuing the program or letting CHIP funding expire.[29]

Extending Federal CHIP Funding

If Congress decides to extend federal CHIP funding after FY2017, there are a number of policy options regarding how long to extend funding and whether to make programmatic changes. Funding could be extended for just a few years (e.g., two or four years) or indefinitely, and the extension could maintain, phase down, or eliminate the 23 percentage point increase to the E-FMAP rate (i.e., the federal matching rate for CHIP). (See the textbox "Federal Cost of Extending CHIP Funding" for more information about extending CHIP funding.)

Federal Cost of Extending CHIP Funding

The Congressional Budget Office (CBO) is required to assume that mandatory spending programs in existence on or before the enactment of the Balanced Budget Act of 1997 (P.L. 105-33), which would include CHIP, that lack future appropriations and have current-year outlays of at least $50 million will continue operating as they had been immediately prior to their expiration. This requirement is in the Balanced Budget and

Emergency Deficit Control Act of 1985, Section 257(b)(2).

Under current law, as shown in Figure 4, funding for CHIP in FY2017 consists of two semiannual appropriations of $2.85 billion—amounts that are much smaller than the appropriations in other years. The first semiannual appropriation in FY2017 will be supplemented by a one-time appropriation in the amount of $14.70 billion provided in the first six months of FY2017 that will remain available until expended. To calculate the CHIP program levels that will continue in the baseline pursuant to these scorekeeping rules, CBO annualizes the $2.85 billion provided for the allotment for the last six months of its authorization for the remainder of the baseline period. CBO does not include the other amounts provided to CHIP for the earlier part of FY2017 because these are not available immediately before the program expires at the end of the fiscal year. For this reason, CBO's baseline for CHIP includes $5.7 billion in federal CHIP funding for each year after FY2017.

FY2017 Funding	
First Six Months	
Semiannual Appropriation	$2.85
One-Time Appropriation	14.70
Second Six Months	
Semiannual Appropriation	$2.85
One-Time Appropriation	+0.0
TOTAL	**$21.06**

CBO Baseline for FY2018 and Subsequent Years	
FY2017 Funding for the Second Six Months	$2.85
Annualized	x2
TOTAL	**$5.70**

Source: Congressional Research Service.
CHIP: State Children's Health Insurance Program.
CBO: Congressional Budget Office.

Figure 4. Federal CHIP Funding for FY2017 and CBO's Baseline for FY2018 and SubsequentYears ($ in billions).

Because the baseline projections assume $5.7 billion in federal CHIP spending for FY2018 and subsequent years within the budget window, CBO's estimated cost of extending federal CHIP funding is lower than it would have been without this assumption. In addition, the federal costs of extending CHIP funding would be offset by reductions in federal spending for Medicaid and subsidized exchange coverage because some CHIP children would receive Medicaid coverage or subsidized exchange coverage if CHIP were to expire.

According to CBO and the Joint Committee on Taxation, the extension of CHIP included in P.L. 114-10 would increase outlays by a net of $5.6 billion over the next 10 years, even with the 23 percentage point increase in the EFMAP rate.[30]

If Federal CHIP Funding Expires

Although FY2017 is the last year for which federal CHIP funding is provided under current law, states are expected to have federal CHIP spending in FY2018 because states will have access to unspent funds from their FY2017 allotments and to unspent FY2016 allotments redistributed to shortfall states (if any).

If federal CHIP funding expires after FY2017, the loss of funding and the ACA MOE requirements would impact states' CHIP programs differently depending on whether the program is a CHIP Medicaid expansion or a separate CHIP program.

The CHIP enrollees in CHIP Medicaid expansion programs (roughly half of CHIP enrollees)[31] likely would continue to receive coverage through their state's Medicaid program due to the ACA MOE requirement, which requires states to maintain income eligibility levels for CHIP children through September 30, 2019, as a condition for receiving any Medicaid funding (notwithstanding the lack of corresponding federal CHIP appropriations for FY2018 and FY2019).[32] This switch would cause the federal share of expenditures to decrease from the E-FMAP rate to the regular FMAP rate, which means the cost of covering these children would increase for states.

For the roughly half of CHIP enrollees in separate CHIP programs,[33] if CHIP funding expires, states would have to enroll these children in Medicaid or certified qualified health plans in the health insurance exchanges.[34] However, if no certified qualified health plans exist, states are relieved from the MOE requirement to provide coverage for the CHIP enrollees in separate CHIP programs when the federal CHIP funding expires.

End Notes

[1] For more information about the State Children's Health Insurance Program (CHIP), see CRS Report R43627, *State Children's Health Insurance Program: An Overview*, by Evelyne P. Baumrucker and Alison Mitchell.

[2] For more information about the impact of the Patient Protection and Affordable Care Act's (ACA's) child maintenance of effort (MOE) provision on CHIP, see CRS Report R43909, *CHIP and the ACA Maintenance of Effort (MOE) Requirement: In Brief*, by Alison Mitchell and Evelyne P. Baumrucker.

[3] For example, assume a state has a federal medical assistance percentage (FMAP) rate of 60%, which means the state share is 40%. To figure out the enhanced federal medical assistance percentage (E-FMAP) rate for this state, first figure out 30% of the state share (i.e., 40%), which is 12%, then subtract 12 percentage points from the state share under Medicaid to get the state share under CHIP, which is 28%. To get the E-FMAP rate, take 100% minus the state share under CHIP to get an E-FMAP rate of 72%.

[4] §2105(b) of the Social Security Act.

[5] States that already had a federal approval plan or that had enacted a state law to submit a plan for federal approval on the date of enactment for the Children's Health Insurance Program Reauthorization Act (CHIPRA; P.L. 111-3). Two states (New Jersey and New York) plus one county in California fall into these exceptions and receive the E-FMAP rate for CHIP enrollees above 300% of the federal poverty level (FPL). No other state provides CHIP coverage to children over 300% of FPL.

[6] The five territories are American Samoa, Guam, the Commonwealth of the Northern Mariana Islands, Puerto Rico, and the Virgin Islands.

[7] The FY2017 appropriation is the combination of two half-year appropriations of $2.85 billion from §2104(a) of the Social Security Act plus a one-time appropriation in the amount of $14.70 billion from §301(b)(3) of the Medicare Access and CHIP Reauthorization Act of 2015 (MACRA; P.L. 114-10).

[8] For more information about the changes enacted under MACRA, see CRS Report R43962, *H.R. 2: The Medicare Access and CHIP Reauthorization Act of 2015*, coordinated by Jim Hahn and Kirstin B. Blom.

[9] From FY2002 through FY2008, the national appropriation amounts were insufficient to cover the full cost of some states' CHIP programs. For FY2002 through FY2005, the amount of redistribution funds from other states was enough to make up the difference. For FY2006 through FY2008, however, additional CHIP appropriations were provided to cover the cost of the federal share of CHIP expenditures.

[12] CHIP Medicaid expansion states may use federal Medicaid funds to pay for CHIP administrative expenditures.

[13] §2104(n) of the Social Security Act.

[14] For Child Enrollment Contingency Fund payments, a state has a funding shortfall if a state's current-year CHIP allotment plus any unused CHIP allotment funds from the previous year are insufficient to cover the federal share of the state's CHIP program. The definition of shortfall funding for Child Enrollment Contingency Fund payments does not factor in redistribution funds.

[15] The target enrollment level for Child Enrollment Contingency Fund payments is the target enrollment level for the previous year increased by the child population growth factor used to calculate the allotment growth factor.

[16] In FY2011, Iowa had a projected shortfall in federal CHIP funding of $3.8 million. Because Iowa's CHIP enrollment exceeded the target level, Iowa was eligible for Child Enrollment Contingency Fund payments and received $28.9 million. (Medicaid and CHIP Payment and Access Commission, *MAC Basics: Federal CHIP Financing*, September 2011; Communication with the Centers for Medicare & Medicaid Services in November 2014.)

[17] §2104(f) of the Social Security Act.

[18] In FY2012 and FY2013, Puerto Rico received $23.7 million and $0.8 million, respectively, in CHIP redistribution funds. (Communication with the Centers for Medicare & Medicaid Services in November 2014.)

[19] Prior to CHIPRA, children in a CHIP Medicaid expansion program were to be paid for out of CHIP funds at the EFMAP rate and Medicaid funding for these children could not be used until a state's available CHIP funding was exhausted. CHIPRA gave states the option to draw Medicaid funds at the regular FMAP rate for CHIP Medicaid expansion children prior to exhausting federal CHIP funding.

[20] The Centers for Medicare & Medicaid Services granted approval for Pennsylvania to delay the transition of CHIP children aged 6 to 18 in families with income less than 133% of FPL until CY2015.

[21] Centers for Medicare & Medicaid Services, "Medicaid Program; Eligibility Changes Under the Affordable Care Act of 2010," 77 *Federal Register* 17144, March 23, 2012; Centers for Medicare & Medicaid Services, *Medicaid and CHIP FAQs: Funding for New Adult Group, Coverage of Former Foster Care Children and CHIP Financing*, December 2013.

[22] MAGI is defined as the Internal Revenue Code's (IRC's) adjusted gross income (AGI) plus certain foreign-earned income and tax-exempt interest. AGI reflects a number of deductions, including trade and business deductions, losses from sale of property, and alimony payments, increased by tax-exempt interest and income earned by U.S. citizens or residents living abroad.

[23] For more information about MAGI, see CRS Report R43861, *The Use of Modified Adjusted Gross Income (MAGI) in Federal Health Programs*, coordinated by Evelyne P. Baumrucker.

[24] Coverage for this population will be paid for out of the state's CHIP allotment at the E-FMAP rate and will cease when the last child has been afforded 12 months of coverage (expected to be no later than April 1, 2016). (Centers for Medicare & Medicaid Services, "Medicaid Program; Eligibility Changes Under the Affordable Care Act of 2010," 77 *Federal Register* 17144, March 23, 2012; Centers for Medicare & Medicaid Services, *Medicaid and CHIP FAQs: Funding for New Adult Group, Coverage of Former Foster Care Children and CHIP Financing*, December 2013.)

[25] Insure Kids Now, *CHIPRA Performance Bonuses: A History*, December 2013.

[26] See Tricia Brooks, Martha Heberlein, and Joseph Fu, Georgetown University Health Policy Institute, Center for Children and Families, *Dismantling CHIP in Arizona: How Losing KidsCare Impacts a Child's Health Care Costs,* May 2014; and Anita Cardwell, et al., National Academy for State Health Policy and Georgetown University Health Policy Institute, Center for Children and Families; *Benefits and Cost Sharing in Separate CHIP Programs*, May 2014.

[27] Under CHIP and Medicaid, out-of-pocket spending (including both premiums and cost sharing) is exempt for many children and pregnant women and, when premiums and cost sharing apply, they cannot exceed 5% of the family's income. For the health insurance exchanges, in 2014, out-of-pocket spending cannot exceed $6,350 for self-only coverage and $12,700 for coverage other than self-only.

[28] Medicaid and CHIP Payment and Access Commission (MACPAC), *Report to Congress on Medicaid and CHIP*, June 2014; Tricia Brooks, "MACPAC Considers Future of CHIP," *Say Ahhh!: A Children's Health Policy* Blog, Georgetown University Health Policy Institute's Center for

Children and Families, November 22, 2013, at http://ccf.georgetown. Edu /all/macpac-considers-future-of-chip/.

[29] The policy options discussed herein reflect current law. They do not take into consideration the potential implications on the ACA coverage provisions from the forthcoming U.S. Supreme Court ruling in King v. Burwell or new legislation. For more information on the potential implications of the Court's decision in King v. Burwell, see CRS Report R43833, *Premium Tax Credits and Federal Health Insurance Exchanges: Questions and Answers*, by Jennifer A. Staman et al.

[30] Congressional Budget Office, Letter to the Honorable John A. Boehner, Re: Cost Estimate and Supplemental Analyses for H.R. 2, the Medicare Access and CHIP Reauthorization Act of 2015, March 25, 2015, at https://www.cbo.gov/sites/default/files/cbofiles/attachments/hr2.pdf.

[31] Preliminary FY2014 CHIP enrollment data show about half of CHIP enrollees are in CHIP Medicaid expansion programs and about half are in separate CHIP programs. See MACPAC, *Report to Congress on Medicaid and CHIP*, March 2015.

[32] For more information about the ACA MOE requirement, see CRS Report R43909, *CHIP and the ACA Maintenance of Effort (MOE) Requirement: In Brief*, by Alison Mitchell and Evelyne P. Baumrucker.

[33] See footnote 31.

[34] A certified qualified health plan is a qualified health plan that has been certified by the Secretary of Health and Human Services to be "at least comparable" to CHIP in terms of benefits and cost sharing.

In: State Children's Health Insurance Program ISBN: 978-1-63483-675-3
Editor: Marty Sparks

Chapter 4

CHIP AND THE ACA MAINTENANCE OF EFFORT (MOE) REQUIREMENT: IN BRIEF*

Alison Mitchell and Evelyne P. Baumrucker

SUMMARY

State Children's Health Insurance Program (CHIP) is a means-tested program that provides health coverage to targeted low-income children and pregnant women in families that have annual income above Medicaid eligibility levels but do not have health insurance. CHIP is jointly financed by the federal government and the states and administered by the states. The federal government sets basic requirements for CHIP, but states have the flexibility to design their own version of CHIP within the federal government's basic framework. States may design their CHIP programs in three ways: a CHIP Medicaid expansion, a separate CHIP program, or a combination approach in which the state operates a CHIP Medicaid expansion and one or more separate CHIP programs concurrently. As a result, there is significant variation across CHIP programs. In FY2013, CHIP enrollment totaled 8.4 million and federal and state CHIP expenditures totaled $13.2 billion.

Under the CHIP statute, FY2017 is the last year federal CHIP funding is provided, even though the Patient Protection and Affordable Care Act (ACA; P.L. 111-148, as amended) child maintenance of effort (MOE)

* This is an edited, reformatted and augmented version of a Congressional Research Service publication R43909, prepared for Members and Committees of Congress dated April 23, 2015.

requirement is in place through FY2019. The MOE provision requires states to maintain income eligibility levels for CHIP children through September 30, 2019, as a condition for receiving federal Medicaid payments (notwithstanding the lack of corresponding federal CHIP appropriations for FY2018 and FY2019). The MOE requirement impacts CHIP Medicaid expansion programs and separate CHIP programs differently.

- *For CHIP Medicaid expansion programs*, when federal CHIP funding is exhausted, the CHIP-eligible children in these programs will continue to be enrolled in Medicaid but financing will switch from CHIP to Medicaid.
- *For separate CHIP programs*, states are provided a couple of exceptions to the MOE requirement: (1) states may impose waiting lists or enrollment caps to limit CHIP expenditures, and (2) after September 1, 2015, states may enroll CHIP-eligible children in qualified health plans in the health insurance exchanges. In addition, in the event that a state's CHIP allotment is insufficient to fund CHIP coverage for all eligible children, a state must establish procedures to screen children for Medicaid eligibility and enroll those who are Medicaid eligible. For children not eligible for Medicaid, the state must establish procedures to enroll CHIP children in qualified health plans in the health insurance exchanges that have been certified by the Secretary of Health and Human Services to be "at least comparable" to CHIP in terms of benefits and cost sharing.

This report discusses the ACA MOE requirement for children if federal CHIP funding expires. It begins with a brief background about CHIP, including information regarding program design and financing. The report then describes the ACA child MOE requirements for CHIP Medicaid expansion programs and for separate CHIP programs and discusses potential coverage implications.

INTRODUCTION

Under the State Children's Health Insurance Program (CHIP) statute, FY2017 is the last year federal CHIP funding is provided, even though the Patient Protection and Affordable Care Act (ACA; P.L. 111-148, as amended) child maintenance of effort (MOE) requirement is in place through FY2019. The ACA MOE provision requires states to maintain income eligibility levels for CHIP children through September 30, 2019, as a condition for receiving federal Medicaid payments (notwithstanding the lack of corresponding federal CHIP appropriations for FY2018 and FY2019).

This report discusses the ACA MOE requirement for children if federal CHIP funding expires. It begins with a brief background of CHIP, including information regarding program design and financing. The report then describes the ACA child MOE requirements for CHIP Medicaid expansion programs and for separate CHIP programs and discusses potential coverage implications.

CHIP Background

CHIP is a federal-state program that provides health coverage to certain uninsured, low-income children and pregnant women in families that have annual income above Medicaid eligibility levels but do not have health insurance.[1] CHIP is jointly financed by the federal government and the states and is administered by the states. Participation in CHIP is voluntary, and all states and the District of Columbia participate. The federal government sets basic requirements for CHIP, but states have the flexibility to design their own version of CHIP within the federal government's basic framework. As a result, there is significant variation across CHIP programs. In FY2013, CHIP enrollment totaled 8.4 million and federal and state CHIP expenditures totaled $13.2 billion.[2]

CHIP was established as part of the Balanced Budget Act of 1997 (P.L. 105-33) under a new Title XXI of the Social Security Act. Since that time, other federal laws have provided additional funding and made significant changes to CHIP. Most notably, the Children's Health Insurance Program Reauthorization Act of 2009 (P.L. 111-3) increased appropriation levels for CHIP, changed the formula for distributing CHIP funding among states, and altered the eligibility and benefit requirements.[3] The ACA largely maintains the current CHIP structure through FY2019 and requires states to maintain their Medicaid and CHIP child eligibility levels through FY2019 as a condition for receiving federal Medicaid matching funds. The ACA provided federal CHIP funding for FY2014 and FY2015, then the Medicare Access and CHIP Reauthorization Act of 2015 (MACRA; P.L. 114-10) extended federal CHIP funding for another two years (i.e., through FY2017).[4]

Program Design

States may design their CHIP programs in three ways: a CHIP Medicaid expansion, a separate CHIP program, or a combination approach in which the state operates a CHIP Medicaid expansion and one or more separate CHIP programs concurrently.

CHIP benefit coverage and cost-sharing rules depend on program design. CHIP Medicaid expansions must follow the federal Medicaid rules for benefits and cost sharing, which entitle CHIP enrollees to Early and Periodic Screening, Diagnostic, and Treatment (EPSDT) coverage (effectively eliminating any state-defined limits on the amount, duration, and scope of any benefit listed in Medicaid statute) and exempt the majority of children from any cost sharing. For separate CHIP programs, states can design benefits that look more like private health insurance and may impose cost sharing, such as premiums or co-payments, with a maximum allowable amount that is tied to annual family income. Aggregate cost sharing under CHIP may not exceed 5% of annual family income.

Regardless of the choice of program design, all states must cover emergency services; well-baby and well-child care, including age-appropriate immunizations; and dental services. If offered, mental health services must meet federal mental health parity requirements. States that want to make changes to their programs beyond what Medicaid or CHIP laws allow may seek approval from the Centers for Medicare & Medicaid Services (CMS) through the use of the Section 1115 waiver authority.[5]

Eight states, the District of Columbia, and the territories had CHIP Medicaid expansions as of July 1, 2014, whereas 13 states had separate CHIP programs[6] and 29 states used a combination approach.[7] According to preliminary CHIP enrollment data for FY2014, about half of CHIP enrollees are in CHIP Medicaid expansion programs and about half are in separate CHIP programs.[8]

CHIP Financing

CHIP is jointly financed by the federal government and the states,[9] with the federal government paying about 70% of total CHIP expenditures.[10] The federal government reimburses states for a portion of every dollar they spend on CHIP (including both CHIP Medicaid expansions and separate CHIP programs) up to state-specific annual limits called allotments. The federal government's share of CHIP expenditures (including both services and administration) is determined by the enhanced federal medical assistance percentage (E-FMAP) rate. The E-FMAP rate is calculated by reducing the state share under the federal medical assistance percentage (FMAP) rate (i.e., the federal matching rate for most Medicaid expenditures) by 30%, which increases the federal share of expenditures.[11] The E-FMAP rate varies by state. In FY2015, the EFMAP rate ranges from 65% (in 13 states) to 82% (in Mississippi). Starting in FY2016, the EFMAP rate is to increase by 23 percentage points for most CHIP expenditures. This increase is to be in effect through FY2019.

Although FY2017 is the last year states are to receive CHIP allotments, federal CHIP outlays are expected in FY2018 because states will have access to unspent funds from their FY2017 allotments and unspent FY2016 allotments redistributed to shortfall states (if any).[12]

In a few situations, federal CHIP funding is used to finance Medicaid expenditures. For instance, certain states significantly expanded Medicaid eligibility for children prior to the enactment of CHIP in 1997.[13] These states are allowed to use their CHIP allotment funds to finance the difference between the Medicaid and CHIP matching rates (i.e., the FMAP and E-FMAP rates, respectively) to cover the cost of children in Medicaid above 133% of the federal poverty level (FPL).[14]

In addition, states may use CHIP allotment funds and receive the higher CHIP matching rate (i.e., E-FMAP rate) for two ACA provisions that went into effect on January 1, 2014:[15] (1) expenditures for children aged 6 to 18 in families with annual income up to 133% of FPL who had been enrolled in separate CHIP programs and were transitioned to Medicaid,[16] and (2) children who moved from CHIP to Medicaid due to the application of the 5% income disregard.[17]

MOE REQUIREMENT

The ACA extended and expanded the MOE provisions in the American Recovery and Reinvestment Act of 2009 (ARRA; P.L. 111-5).[18] The ACA MOE provisions contain separate requirements for Medicaid and CHIP and were designed to ensure that individuals eligible for these programs did not lose coverage between the date of enactment of the ACA (March 23, 2010) and the implementation of the health insurance exchanges (for adults) and September 30, 2019 (for children).

Under the ACA MOE provisions, states are required to maintain their Medicaid programs with the same eligibility standards, methodologies, and procedures in place on the date of enactment of the ACA until January 1, 2014, for adults and through September 30, 2019, for children up to the age of 19. The ACA also requires states to maintain income eligibility levels for CHIP children through September 30, 2019, as a condition for receiving payments under Medicaid.[19] The penalty to states for not complying with either the Medicaid or the CHIP MOE requirements would be the loss of all federal Medicaid matching funds.[20]

Together, these MOE requirements for Medicaid and CHIP impact CHIP Medicaid expansion programs and separate CHIP programs differently.[21]

CHIP Medicaid Expansion Programs

For CHIP Medicaid expansion programs, the Medicaid and CHIP MOE provisions apply concurrently.[22] For states to continue to receive federal Medicaid funds, the ACA child MOE provisions require that CHIP-eligible children in CHIP Medicaid expansion programs must continue to be eligible for Medicaid through September 30, 2019.[23] When a state's federal CHIP funding is exhausted, the state's financing for these children switches from CHIP to Medicaid. This switch would cause the state share of covering these children to increase because the federal matching rate for Medicaid is less than the E-FMAP rate.

As discussed above, states may have some Medicaid expenditures financed with federal CHIP funds. In any of these situations, when federal CHIP funding is exhausted, states would be responsible for continuing to provide Medicaid coverage to these children through September 30, 2019. However, as is the case with the CHIP Medicaid expansion programs, the financing would switch from CHIP to Medicaid, resulting in an increase in the state share of these expenditures because the federal matching rate would be lowered from the E-FMAP rate to the FMAP rate.

Separate CHIP Programs

For separate CHIP programs, only the CHIP-specific provisions of the ACA MOE requirements are applicable. These provisions contain a couple of exceptions:

1. states may impose waiting lists or enrollment caps to limit CHIP expenditures, or
2. after September 1, 2015, states may enroll CHIP-eligible children in qualified health plans in the health insurance exchanges that have been certified by the Secretary of Health and Human Services (HHS) to be "at least comparable" to CHIP in terms of benefits and cost sharing.

In addition, in the event that a state's CHIP allotment is insufficient to fund CHIP coverage for all eligible children, a state must establish procedures to screen CHIP-eligible children for Medicaid eligibility[24] and to enroll those who are eligible in Medicaid.

For children not eligible for Medicaid, the state must establish procedures to enroll CHIP-eligible children in qualified health plans offered in the health insurance exchanges that have been certified by the Secretary of HHS to be "at least comparable" to CHIP in terms of benefits and cost sharing. Under these ACA MOE requirements, states are required only to establish procedures to enroll children in qualified health plans certified by the Secretary. If there are no certified plans, the MOE requirement does not obligate states to provide coverage to these children. Even when there are certified plans, not all CHIP children may be eligible for subsidized exchange coverage due to the *family glitch*,[25] among other reasons.

CONCLUSION

FY2017 is the last year federal CHIP funding is provided in the CHIP statute. If no additional federal funding is provided for the program, once federal CHIP funding is exhausted, CHIP children in CHIP Medicaid expansion programs would continue to receive coverage under Medicaid through at least FY2019, due to the ACA MOE requirement. However, coverage of CHIP children in separate CHIP programs who are not eligible for Medicaid depends on the availability of qualified health plans that are certified by the Secretary of HHS to be "at least comparable" to CHIP in terms of benefits and cost sharing unless states decide to provide state-funded CHIP coverage.

End Notes

[1] For more information about the State Children's Health Insurance Program (CHIP), see CRS Report R43627, State Children's Health Insurance Program: An Overview, by Evelyne P. Baumrucker and Alison Mitchell.

[2] Medicaid and CHIP Payment and Access Commission, Report to Congress on Medicaid and CHIP, March 2014.

[3] For more information on the changes enacted under the Children's Health Insurance Program Reauthorization Act of 2009, see CRS Report R40226, P.L. 111-3: The Children's Health Insurance Program Reauthorization Act of 2009, by Evelyne P. Baumrucker, Elicia J. Herz, and Jane G. Gravelle.

[4] For more information about the changes enacted under the Medicare Access and CHIP Reauthorization Act of 2015 (MACRA; P.L. 114-10), see CRS Report R43962, H.R. 2: The Medicare Access and CHIP Reauthorization Act of 2015, coordinated by Jim Hahn and Kirstin B. Blom.

[5] Under §1115 of the Social Security Act, the Secretary of Health and Human Services (HHS) may waive CHIP program requirements so states can test new program design options that further the goals of the CHIP program. CHIP §1115 waivers are time limited (up to five years) and must be allotment neutral to the federal government. In other words, they cannot cost the federal government more than what is available under the state's annual allotment(s) (i.e., federal funds allocated to each state for the federal share of its CHIP expenditures) applicable to the fiscal years for which the demonstration is operational.

[6] As of July 1, 2014, 2 states (Washington and Connecticut) had separate CHIP programs with no Medicaid expansions. The remaining 11 states (Alabama, Arizona, Georgia, Kansas, Oregon, Mississippi, Pennsylvania, Texas, Utah, West Virginia, and Wyoming) are considered to have separate CHIP programs, but technically these programs are part of combination CHIP programs due to the ACA requirement to transition CHIP children aged 6 through 18 in families with annual income less than 133% of the federal poverty level (based on modified adjusted gross income, or MAGI) to Medicaid, beginning January 1, 2014.

[7] Centers for Medicare & Medicaid Services (CMS), Children's Health Insurance Program Plan Activity, as of July 1, 2014.

[8] Medicaid and CHIP Payment and Access Commission, Report to the Congress on Medicaid and CHIP, March 2015.

[9] For more information about federal CHIP financing, see CRS Report R43949, Federal Financing for the State Children's Health Insurance Program (CHIP), by Alison Mitchell.

[10] U.S. Department of Health and Human Services, CMS, Form CMS-64 data.

[11] For more information about the federal medical assistance percentage (FMAP) rate and how it is calculated, see CRS Report R43847, Medicaid's Federal Medical Assistance Percentage (FMAP), FY2016, by Alison Mitchell.

[12] If a state's CHIP allotment for the current year, in addition to any allotment funds carried over from the prior year, is insufficient to cover the projected CHIP expenditures for the current year, a few different shortfall funding sources are available. These include Child Enrollment Contingency Funds, redistribution funds, and Medicaid funds.

[13] The following 11 states meet this definition: Connecticut, Hawaii, Maryland, Minnesota, New Hampshire, New Mexico, Rhode Island, Tennessee, Vermont, Washington, and Wisconsin.

[14] §2015(g) of the Social Security Act.

[15] CMS, "Medicaid and CHIP FAQs: Funding for New Adult Group, Coverage of Former Foster Care Children and CHIP Financing," December 2013.

[16] The E-FMAP rate is not available for children aged 6 to 18 who have access to private health insurance.

[17] Beginning January 1, 2014, the ACA required the federal government and states to rely on MAGI rules when determining eligibility for CHIP, Medicaid (for most nonelderly populations), and subsidized exchange coverage. Under MAGI rules, a state looks at each individual's MAGI, deducts 5% (which the law provides as a standard disregard), and compares that income with the new income standards set by each state.

[18] The American Recovery and Reinvestment Act of 2009 (ARRA; P.L. 111-5; extended in P.L. 111-226) included a temporary increase in the FMAP. To receive the FMAP increase under ARRA, states were required to maintain the same Medicaid eligibility standards, methodologies, and procedures in effect on July 1, 2008, through June 30, 2011.

[19] §2105(d)(3) of the Social Security Act.

[20] §1902(gg)(2) of the Social Security Act.

[21] The Secretary of HHS has not issued guidance regarding the impact of the maintenance of effort (MOE) requirements if federal CHIP funding expires.

[22] Both the CHIP child MOE requirement and the Medicaid child MOE requirement concurrently apply to the CHIP Medicaid expansion programs.

[23] CHIP children covered under CHIP Medicaid expansion programs are an optional eligibility group under Medicaid. However, because the Medicaid MOE for children extends through FY2019, states are not permitted to roll back Medicaid eligibility for these children without the loss of all Medicaid federal matching funds.

[24] States must conduct eligibility redeterminations for Medicaid and CHIP at least annually. Due to fluctuations in income among the CHIP target population, it is possible that a formerly CHIP-eligible child may meet the state's Medicaid eligibility standard due to a change in annual income that may not have been taken into consideration until the enrollee's next regularly scheduled eligibility redetermination.

[25] Subsidized coverage in the health insurance exchanges is not available to individuals with access to affordable health insurance. The family glitch results from the definition of affordable coverage. Under the ACA, employer-sponsored insurance is considered affordable if an employee's premium contributions for self-only coverage (not family coverage) comprise less than 9.5% of household income. However, there is no affordability limit on the employee's share of the premium for family coverage. Due to the family glitch, some current CHIP enrollees would not be eligible for subsidized coverage in the health insurance exchanges based on a parent's access to affordable employer-sponsored insurance. For more information about subsidized coverage in the health insurance exchanges, see CRS Report R41137, Health Insurance Premium Credits in the Patient Protection and Affordable Care Act (ACA) in 2014, by Bernadette Fernandez.

INDEX

C

D

N

O

P

Q

R

S